COVET
THE COMEBACK

CHRISTOS GARKINOS

How a Son of Greek Immigrants Found Success,
Lost Everything, Then Built a Fashion Empire

Advance Praise for Covet the Comeback

"In his un-put-down-able memoir, Christos Garkinos takes us on a gripping journey from a Greek diner in Detroit to the heights of the fashion world. Christos shares his struggles and triumphs, weaving a narrative rich with cultural heritage and the relentless pursuit of the American dream. I'm proud to say that my best friend of 20 years has created a masterpiece that will make you laugh, cry and hope. *Covet the Comeback* is a must-read for anyone who believes in the power of second chances and the magic of following your passion."

—Garcelle Beauvais, actress, producer, television host and bestselling author

Contents

For Nick the Greek and Aspasia—lovingly looking down on me from heaven—telling me to get my butt back to work!

Preface

Picture it: It's the dawn of the Swingin' Seventies and you're headed to lunch at Meat Town, Metro Detroit's finest Greek diner, where the chain-smoking, cocktail-swilling Nick the Greek, who looks less like a cook and more like a movie star, is working the grill, sending out steaks the way he wants to cook them. As the sign out front says, "This Ain't No Burger King": Here, meat is served Nick's way or no way. If you've got any complaints, leave them with the seven-year-old kid working the register. He'll be happy to direct you over to his dad—if you're interested in being screamed at in Greek and then thrown out of the joint.

That kid, as you've probably guessed by now, is me—but I've come a long way from Meat Town.

Over the last 50 years, I've worked for some of the biggest companies in entertainment (for one very famous mouse and for the world's nicest, coolest billionaire, to name a few), become an accidental reality TV star, launched a wildly successful clothing line on

HSN and literally dug through the closets of every celebrity you can imagine.

Vogue Japan called me one of the most fashionable men in the world, and I've also driven around LA in a Range Rover wondering if I was going to make next month's rent.

I've met everyone you've ever wanted to meet and launched the revolutionary Covet by Christos luxury goods live streaming network, where I have brought everything I've learned from a career working in fashion, business and TV to social media. Since 2020 alone, I've sold over $100 millions of dollars' worth of luxury goods on the network. I've done a lot, is what I'm trying to say, and I've lost—and found—love, friendships and careers along the way. I've said goodbye to some of the biggest loves of my life, and I've learned to both process loss and to understand that those who leave us never really leave us.

It's hard to make it to the top and it's hard to stay on top, but what it's *really* hard to do is make a comeback.

I've done it—more than once—and, of everything I've experienced, that's what I'm most proud of. If I could offer you one piece of advice, it's this: don't covet designer shoes, celebrity-filled parties or even the kind of fame that comes with people wanting to hug you on the street. What I really think you should covet is the comeback, and in the following pages, I'm going to do my best to show you why—and how.

I'm not saying I know it all, but along the way I've made some mistakes, learned some hard lessons and figured out that my best bet is the one I made on myself.

I'm ready to get into the good, the bad and the ugly here, even when it involves me getting hit in the face with a tetherball and falling off a chair in front of Sophia Loren.

If only Nick the Greek could see me now...

...he'd tell me to quit wasting time and get my ass back to work.

Chapter 1

Another day, another recess spent on the playground of Ferry Elementary School...alone.

Another cold Michigan winter spent zipped up in my practical, warm brown coat pondering some of life's most eternal questions:

Why do I feel so different from all the other kids?

Am I ever going to get out of Michigan?

Who am I, and what's waiting out there for me?

I was playing tetherball, that time-honored sport of friendless kids. Just me, the pole and a ball on a string, going around and around in a circle until the bell rang and it was time to go back to class. I was mid-thwack when I heard the sound that would change my life forever: Click, clack. Click, clack. Someone—A teacher? A mom? A mysterious jewel thief disguised as a teacher or a mom in Grosse Pointe, Michigan?—was walking down the sidewalk adjacent to the playground in a pair of high heels, and the sound they made on the concrete unlocked something in me.

It was the sound of glamor. The sound of Hollywood starlets walking down the red carpet and across soundstages in California. The sound of a New York City heiress crossing the room at a cocktail party to say hello to an ambassador from Paris and a fashion designer from Milan. It was about as far as you can get from suburban Detroit, and in that moment, I knew that was where I was going to go. No more practical brown coats for me. I was going to grow up, get out of Grosse Pointe and become a star—or at least someone who hung out with stars.

Lost in the reverie of my future life, I saw myself traveling the world in first class, jetting off to the South of France just because I could, using my wits and sense of fashion (I already had one, even if I didn't know it yet) to create a life that felt like those high heels sounded—powerful, glamorous and special. I was mentally decorating my penthouse apartment—should the conversation pit go in the den, or in the living room in front of the floor-to-ceiling windows that faced the downtown skyline? Finally, I was re-tethered to reality—literally, since in my daydreaming, I lost track of the tetherball and it came flying around the pole, whacking me right in the face and leaving me with a black eye I'd have for the next week.

I'd like to say that was the first and last time I'd learn that what comes around goes around, but is it ever that easy?

I guess now I should tell you about how I ended up in Grosse Pointe, which means telling you about my immigrant parents and how *they* ended up in Grosse Pointe, the preppiest city in the world.

From the Old Country to Detroit: A Tale of Two Immigrants

The Garkinos name itself was forged out of my grandfather's remarkable life. He was, by all accounts, a towering, dark-skinned "gypsy" from the rugged mountains of northern Greece, a man whose life was as mysterious as it was legendary in our family. Known for his strength, his resilience and his somewhat dangerous profession, he made his living dynamiting mountains to clear paths for new roads. Each day, he'd saddle up on his striking white horse and travel to his next location, a formidable figure known by all the villagers. Standing at six foot six, he was often called "El Greco," the tall, enigmatic Greek dynamite man whose strength, courage and good looks preceded him.

Our family name, Garkinos, emerged as a tribute to this storied figure, his legend seeping into the identity of every Garkinos born after him. In many ways, our family carried this name like a badge of honor. People recognized "Garkinos" as more than just a surname; it represented resilience, mystery and a certain boldness that defied convention.

This name was more than a moniker; it was a narrative itself, filled with unspoken power. It wasn't tied to a specific village or bound by the usual customs of Greek heritage. Instead, it reflected a kind of nomadic strength, a reminder of my grandfather's wandering spirit, his unbreakable will, and his ability to carve a path through the harshest landscapes. "Garkinos" is a talisman—a grounding symbol of roots, hardships and the relentless pursuit of survival against all odds.

El Greco's son, Nick the Greek, was my father, a man who seemed born to stand out, even among legends. Captured by the Nazis as a young man, he fought in WWII and escaped with his life, though I know—from hearing him wake up screaming in the middle of the night—that the memories of that time never left him. Nick was impossibly good-looking, with bone structure that looked like it had been carved by a Greek sculptor.

Standing at six feet tall, he had chiseled features, a six pack and an aura of quiet, cool confidence that just drew people to him—a real Don Draper type. He looked like the singer Engelbert Humperdinck, except somehow even more handsome. Women were captivated by him, to the point that my mother had to fend them off in the streets. But it wasn't just his looks; it was his style, his presence. My father knew how to put together an outfit like nobody else—velvet tuxedos, double-breasted suits, colors that only he could pull off.

Fashion wasn't something he learned from magazines or television; it was instinctual. He could walk into a room in a mustard velvet jacket, a brightly-colored patterned tie and a perfectly-tailored overcoat and literally stop conversation—that's how good he looked. It was all part of his persona, his own way of expressing himself in a world that didn't always understand him. For him, style was more than appearance; it was a statement of confidence and charisma, and people were naturally drawn to that. His presence lit up every party he went to, and his fashion choices became a symbol of his self-assuredness—he was Nick the Greek and don't you forget it, his affect seemed to say.

Nick the Greek wasn't just a fashion icon; he was also a talented dancer and a social magnet. On the weekends, he and my mother would go out, and together they became the talk of Detroit's Greek Town. They danced like no one else, with my father famously balancing a shot of whiskey on his head, performing backflips and moving with an ease that made people stop and watch. He brought life to every gathering, not just through his presence but through the spirit he infused into those around him.

Watching him dance and live with such energy, I was both captivated and challenged, wondering how I could ever live up to a man who seemed capable of casting his own myth. My father's vivacity extended far beyond his personal life; he brought that same energy to his role in our family. Even in Detroit's Greek Town, a place where everyone was a character and everyone had what seemed like a novel-worthy story, Nick the Greek was someone you wanted to know.

My mom's journey to the Land of Opportunity reads like a bittersweet fairy tale, a story that encapsulates the dreams, struggles and resilience of millions of immigrants who sought a better life on American shores. She was a pretty, dark-eyed 12-year-old girl from a tiny village in Rhodes, Greece, stepping off a boat at Ellis Island in 1947, her eyes wide with a mixture of fear and wonder at what might await her in this new country.

She'd never even met her father before, thanks to a combination of long-distance romance and World War II throwing a wrench in their family plans. Her father, my grandfather, had pulled a classic "love 'em and leave 'em" move during a trip back to Greece, managing to impregnate my grandmother before hopping back across the pond to America. Then World War II hit, and suddenly there was a whole ocean and a global conflict between a father and his unborn child.

For years, letters and the occasional photograph were the only connections between my mother and her father.

Life in her small village was a daily struggle, with my grandmother working tirelessly to provide for her two daughters. The war had only exacerbated their hardships, turning an already challenging life into a constant battle for survival. Most days, they weren't sure where the next meal was coming from or what invading army might show up next. In the tiny island village of Katavia—where Aspasia, aka Bessie, my mother, was growing up—everyone's a cousin. I'm not exaggerating—to this day, I'm still not entirely sure how the family tree branches out, but I'm pretty confident that if you shake it hard enough, a few more cousins will fall out. This close-knit community was both a blessing and a curse. On one hand, there was always someone to lend a helping hand or share a meal. On the other, privacy was pretty much nonexistent, and if my mother had stayed there, her options for fun, excitement and marriage would have been limited, to say the least.

A Match Made in the Bowling Alley

So, how did these two Greek immigrants with their heavy baggage (both literal and emotional) end up together?

Was it a chance meeting at a souvlaki stand? A passionate debate over the best way to wrap a grape leaf? Perhaps a dramatic encounter at a Greek festival, where their eyes met across a crowded dance floor as the bouzouki played in the background?

Nope. Their love story, as it turns out, was far more American than either of them would have guessed, blending the old world with the new in a way that perfectly encapsulated the immigrant experience. They met in the most American way possible: at a bowling alley. The setting for this Greek-American romance was not the sun-drenched shores of the Mediterranean, but the fluorescent-lit lanes of a Detroit bowling alley, where the clash of pins and the squeak of rental shoes provided the soundtrack to their budding love.

The epic love story of Nick and Bess began with the sweet smells of shoe disinfectant and hot French fries. My father, all slicked-back hair and brooding good looks, lining up his shot while my mother, a looker herself, pretended not to notice from two lanes over. It was a meet-cute straight out of a 1950s sitcom, but with a distinctly Greek flavor. It was a classic case of good girl meets Greek god, and all the *yia-yias* were aflutter: would Nick's wild ways be tamed by Bess's gentle influence? Or would Bess be swept off her feet by Nick's irresistible charm?

They were a study in contrasts—the rebel and the

good girl, the risk-taker and the planner—but somehow, against all odds, they just worked.

They had a big fat Greek wedding, and thus began the next chapter of their American dream, though I'd be remiss not to mention that my mom continued to be an *excellent* bowler with over 100 trophies—eliciting groans of "Sit down, Bessie" (a phrase that's become part of my signature lexicon, as we'll get into a little later in the story) from would-be rivals well into her 80s.

Welcome to Meat Town

My father, Hollywood character that he was, wanted to be a hairstylist. He was good with his hands and had a sense of style, so I can see how it would have been a good fit for him. It's easy to close my eyes and imagine him shaping blonde shags on the set of a James Bond movie or cruising over Laurel Canyon in an Italian convertible as he jets between a salon on Rodeo Drive and a celebrity client's house in Benedict Canyon. But, at the end of the day, my father didn't live in Hollywood.

He lived, like so many other Greek immigrants, in Detroit, and he had a wife and a pair of kids to take care of. While my mom worked in insurance for Motown Records and some of soul music's biggest names like Diana Ross and the Supremes, my father turned to the restaurant business.

Nick and Bessie bought the Meat Town Inn, located smack dab in the heart of Detroit's Eastern Market. It was the largest open-air market in the States, a bustling hub of commerce that's been around longer than sliced bread (literally—it's over 100 years old). Eastern Market was, and still is, a microcosm of Detroit's vibrant food culture, where farmers, butchers and restaurateurs converge in a cacophony of sights, smells and tastes from around the world, imported to Michigan and given a Detroit spin.

And right in the middle of this carnivore's paradise, my dad transitioned from meat cutter to restaurant owner faster than you can say "medium rare." It was a bold move, fueled by equal parts ambition and the sheer audacity that comes with being an immigrant determined to make it in America. The Meat Town Inn wasn't a greasy spoon. It was a temple of meat, a sanctuary for carnivores, a place where vegetarians feared to tread (or were converted on the spot by the irresistible aroma of sizzling steaks).

My dad, with his meat-cutting expertise, remade himself as a culinary maestro overnight. He wielded his knives with the precision of a surgeon and the flair of a showman, turning hunks of beef into offerings Zeus himself would've been pleased with.

The menu at Meat Town Inn was a work of art, and by art, I mean it was probably scribbled on a napkin with a stubborn piece of charcoal. It was a testament to simplicity and quality—no fancy French names or pretentious descriptions here. Just good, honest, meat-centric fare with a Greek twist. The piece de resistance? A sign at the door that read: "This Ain't No Burger King. You get it my way or you don't get the goddamn thing."

Gordon Ramsay, eat your heart out. This wasn't just a slogan; it was my dad's philosophy distilled into a single, glorious, grammatically-questionable sentence. It was a declaration of independence from customer whims, a battle cry against the "the customer is always right" mentality.

In Meat Town Inn, the customer was always right... as long as they agreed with my dad, because the Meat Town Inn was about Nick the Greek. He was the star of the show, the reason Greeks and non-Greeks alike came to sip cocktails and eat souvlaki, hoping to catch a glimpse of the handsome, take-no-shit chef.

This was where I got my first taste of the business world, and it was a baptism by fire (or should I say, by grill?). At the ripe old age of five, I was already a regular worker at the restaurant—Greek parents do not obey child labor laws.

My typical day went something like this: Wake up at an ungodly hour (because apparently, the early bird gets the worm, but the early Greek gets the prime cuts), ride to the restaurant with mom, catch some sleep under the bar (because every kid needs a nap nook in a bar, right?), then wake up to the soothing sounds of my mother angrily typing out the lunch menu.

It was a crash course in the restaurant business, complete with the ambient soundtrack of sizzling meat and clanging pots, punctuated by a constant stream of Greek expletives. The restaurant was my playground, my school and sometimes, quite literally, my bedroom. I learned more about life, business and human nature in those early morning hours than I ever did in a classroom, and I attribute much of the hustle that has carried me through my career to these years.

I watched as my parents navigated the treacherous waters of entrepreneurship, dealing with everything from fussy customers to temperamental suppliers, all while trying to maintain that delicate balance between "authentic Greek hospitality" and "don't mess with the cook."

By six years old, I was manning the cash register like a pro. We're talking an old-school, wooden beast of a machine that probably weighed more than I did. It was a monstrosity of gears and levers, a relic from a time when "digital" referred to fingers and toes, not technology. Operating this mechanical marvel was like piloting a steam engine—it required strength, skill and a fair bit of percussive maintenance (read: whacking it when it got stuck).

My math skills? Impeccable. My ability to reach the top of the register without a step stool? Not so much. But what I lacked in height, I made up for in enthusiasm and a knack for charming customers with my precocious business acumen.

I wasn't content to be a humble cashier, though—any kindergartener with half a brain could do that job, I thought. By seven, I had expanded my repertoire to include mixology. While other kids were mixing mud pies in the woods, I was shaking martinis. Child labor laws? Never heard of 'em.

At the Meat Town Inn, if you could see over the bar (or at least reach it on tiptoes), you were qualified to mix drinks. I became a pint-sized Tom Cruise from "Cocktail," minus the hair flips and plus a healthy dose of Greek sass, which the customers loved—they'd expect nothing less from Nick and Bessie's boy. Our idea of quality family time consisted of gathering around giant Budweiser bottles (the four-foot plastic novelty kind, not the drinkable ones) and sorting coins from the day's take. Nothing says "family bonding" quite like the clink of quarters being stuffed into paper rolls, and it was our nightly ritual, a time to recount the day's triumphs and tribulations and, most importantly, the day's earnings.

Restaurants are a cash business, and my parents, both of whom had come from nothing—less than nothing, really—were constantly worried about making money. It rubbed off on me, and even as an adult with my own bank accounts, I still feel that scarcity mindset, the idea that today might be the day people stop wanting to come to Meat Town and order a steak—so I'd better figure out how to pivot.

When I wasn't at Meat Town, I was in the inner city Detroit duplex we lived in, supervised by every Greek in the neighborhood, most of whom we were related to. My *yia-yia and papou* lived below us in our building and my aunts lived down the street, so it felt like the whole block was an extension of my home.

There certainly wasn't much privacy: we had a phone, but it was—as was common back then— run on a party line, which meant you had to pick it up and tell the person five houses down to hang it up so you could make your call. My *yia-yia* was the anchor of our neighborhood, constantly burning herbs and incense and insisting my sister and I run around the table in a special ritual designed to ward off evil spirits.

My First Red Carpet

If home and Meat Town were two pillars of my universe, the third was the Greek Orthodox Church.

Twice a week, I'd trade in my regular classes for lessons in Greek language, history and how to properly shame someone using only our eyebrows. This was a full-blown immersion into Greek culture, complete with stern-faced teachers who seemed to have perfected the art of making you feel guilty for not knowing the proper conjugation of irregular verbs in Ancient Greek.

Greek school was a rite of passage for every Greek-American kid in our community—our parents' and grandparents' way of making sure we grew up not just American, but Greek, too. The real show, though, happened on Sundays, when the whole neighborhood would turn out for church services dressed in their finest clothes. Think quilted leather Chanel bags, pastel pillbox hats a la Jackie Kennedy and candy-colored tweed suits accented with thick ropes of gold necklaces.

The jewels on these Greek ladies would have made Elizabeth Taylor take notice, and they certainly had an impact on me: I think of church as the first time I ever walked a red carpet and I think of the women I'd see each week as some of my first celebrities coming forward to receive communion. I was part of the show, too, as an altar boy, and I have to say, I was a pretty fabulous one.

The outfits were extremely glamorous: we're talking robes that would make any Project Runway contestant weep with envy. Flowing brocade, shimmering gold accents and sashes that could double as superhero capes. Every Sunday was like a haute couture fashion show, with each altar boy trying to outdo the others in how gracefully they could swing the incense burner or how majestically they could carry the oversized Bible.

The process of getting dressed for altar duty was a ritual in itself. We'd gather in the back room of the church, transforming from ordinary Greek-American kids in ill-fitting suits (because you always buy them a size too big to "grow into") into these...ethereal *beings* draped in yards of luxurious fabric. The older boys would help the younger ones, showing us how to properly tie the sashes and adjust the robes for maximum dramatic effect.

It really was like being backstage at a fashion show, only with more incense and less hairspray. There I'd be, holding the cross of Jesus (casual, right?), looking out at the congregation, feeling the cross in my hands, the swish of the robes around my ankles, the eyes of every Greek person in Detroit directly on me. I'd proceed down the aisle, trying my best to look solemn and holy, all while secretly reveling in the drama of it all.

Who knew that the path from altar to atelier was so direct? The church, with all its pomp and ceremony, was unknowingly nurturing my budding sense of style and my love for the impact clothes can have on our lives.

Every Sunday was a lesson in the power of clothing to transform, to elevate, to make the ordinary extraordinary. The attention to detail required in properly arranging the altar, the importance of presentation, the way different fabrics moved and caught the light—these were all early lessons in design and aesthetics. The Greek Orthodox Church, with its rich traditions and visual splendor, was my first classroom in the art of fashion.

Early (and Forever) Icons

At home, too, I was becoming a version of myself I still recognize today: my sister, like any good mid-century American girl, had a vast collection of Barbies, and I, as her older brother, took it upon myself not to play with René's barbies but to style them. This hat went with this dress, and this heel absolutely had to be worn with the matching bag.

In a nod to the entrepreneurial spirit I inherited from my parents, I also loved setting up a Barbie store, an imaginary shop where these blonde dolls could come and get outfitted for skiing or Malibu or date night with Ken.

I loved actual celebrities, too, especially big-haired singers who performed on TV in gold and silver minidresses and platform boots. My parents had a jukebox in the restaurant, and it was, like a lot of things from that era, a mafia-run jukebox. Every two months the mafia people, operating on the orders of the Godfathers, would come and change all the 45s in the jukebox, and once a single's time was up, we'd get to take it home.

As a Detroit boy, I was obsessed with Motown, *especially* Diana Ross and Supremes, for whom I made my family sick. Literally! Kentucky Fried Chicken ran a promotion: if you bought 12 family meals in an extremely short period of time, you got a free three-album set of

Diana Ross and Supremes recordings of their final concert at the Tropicana. At eight years old, I was going to die if I didn't get these records, and I begged my parents to take our family to KFC for dinner...four nights in a row.

We ate so much fried chicken that we all felt terrible, but I got those records. I kept them, too, and 30 years later, I had the pleasure of meeting *the* Mary Wilson of the Supremes and asking her to autograph them for me.

That, in a nutshell, was me as a kid: eager to please, eager to learn, eager to work for what I wanted.

I added up tips, shook up old fashioneds, and idolized pop divas, wishing and hoping, as the song goes, that I was destined for something big. At the very least, I was aiming for a life that didn't include me smacking my own face with a tetherball on a regular basis.

I'm still working on it. I'll keep you posted.

Chapter 2

La Dolce Vita, Christos-Style

The things I wanted as a kid were different from the things other kids wanted. I wasn't begging for a new fishing rod or tickets to a baseball game. My parents weren't ungenerous, so when my birthday rolled around, they asked me how I wanted to celebrate.

"For my birthday I want to go to the mall to meet Sophia Loren," I exclaimed.

They looked at me quizzically; had they heard me right? Sophia Loren was an icon, of course, but she wasn't really an icon for tween boys in suburban Michigan in the early 1980s. I'm sure they wondered, *What would Sophia Loren even be doing in Grosse Pointe?* But I was resolute. Sophia Loren was coming to our local mall to promote her new perfume Sophia, an amber-forward scent with notes of jasmine and rose. It would go on to be one of the first big celebrity perfumes, proving that once again I had my finger on the absolute pulse of good taste.

My parents, to their credit, shrugged their shoulders and said, "Okay, we'll go to the mall to meet Sophia Loren." They probably appreciated that it was cheaper than a fishing rod.

When the big day finally arrived, I dressed, did my hair and gave myself a final once-over as we walked out of the house. On the way to the mall, I practiced in my head. I just knew I was going to meet Sophia, and while I didn't really know where it was going to go from there (Would we become best friends? Would she invite me to Italy to eat handmade pasta and swim in the Adriatic Sea? Would she lobby to get me a cameo in her next movie?), I wasn't worried. I had this in the bag.

When we got there, I realized I wasn't the only person desperate to meet Sophia, though I was probably the youngest by 30 years and definitely the only 12-year-old boy there of his own volition. As the queen of Italian cinema and one of the great beauties of the 20th century walked into the room like she was walking the red carpet at Cannes, she waved to her adoring public, her wig slightly askew and her signature large glasses on the bridge of her nose, scanning the crowd for smiling faces and eager expressions. I climbed up on my folding chair to get a better view and realized as I stood above the crowd that I was now at eye level with the woman who made everyone want to be Italian.

"Sophia," I yelled, willing her to notice me. "Sophia, over here, it's my birthday!" Against all odds, we locked eyes, hers lively and mine filled with longing and admiration. I opened my mouth to shout something else and just as the words were about to come out, I felt the chair slip out from under my feet.

Before I knew what was happening, my body was hitting the hard, cold marble floor of the mall, and my dream of meeting Sophia slipped away as she turned to greet someone else. It was the tetherball incident all over again, but this time I had gotten even closer to my dream before falling on my ass. Hey, it was progress, right?

Adventures in Suburbia, Part I

One day, we got new neighbors and my mother decided we had to move. In retrospect, it had been a long time coming, as Detroit started to get a reputation for being unsafe and my father, who worked in a cash business, was held up several times at the restaurant.

At the time, I was pretty sure we were moving because of our new neighbors and their waterbed. Seriously: I asked my mom if I could go next door and play with Heather on her family's waterbed (actually, I'm going to give this one to Bessie—that does sound kind of weird), and basically the next day, we were packing up our duplex, saying one last goodbye on the party line and moving to a house in Grosse Pointe, an iconic, John Hughes movie-style suburb where the houses were big, people dressed in pink and green, and the schools were good.

The Greeks, more of whom were fleeing the city for the suburbs every day, were a novelty to kids raised on mayonnaise and white bread. My new neighbors literally had names like Buffy and Miffy, and I was pretty sure I was the only member of my new middle-school class who had worked the night shift shaking up martinis for a restaurant filled with hungry, thirsty patrons who demanded the next round before their glasses even hit the table.

Despite the fact that we were far from the only Greek family making the move, in our new town, I was different in a way I hadn't experienced before. In Detroit, I was just another Greek kid in a sea of Greek kids. In Grosse Pointe, I might as well have been from another planet.

My olive skin, my "exotic" lunches, my large, loud family—everything about me seemed to scream "other" in this new environment. I was too smart, too ethnic, too sensitive. I cried easily, which only made the bullying worse. Every day felt like a battle, trying to navigate this new social landscape while also grappling with my emerging identity.

Enter Louis Theros, my unlikely knight in shining armor. Louis's Greek parents were friends with mine, which meant he was basically stuck with me. He tried valiantly to protect me from the relentless onslaught of playground bullies, but when you're facing a gang of 10-year-olds, even the best intentions can fall flat.

I spent a lot of my time alone, which is why I became the reigning champion of tetherball (you know, minus hitting my own face with the ball). As the weeks wore on, I settled into a routine of sorts. I became the quintessential teacher's pet, a role I wore as a badge of honor. The teachers loved me, and I basked in their praise, happy someone thought I was worth paying attention to. I was the kid who raised his hand too eagerly, brought in cookies for the class and had a crush on Mr. La Salla, my fifth-grade teacher.

Mr. La Salla was a towering figure with a mustache that looked like it had been borrowed from a 1970s cop show—a dead ringer for Tom Selleck. He had a pack of Marlboro Reds in his pocket, which only added to his rugged charm. I often fantasized about impressing him with my knowledge of the periodic table, but in reality, I was just trying to make it through the day without getting my lunch money stolen.

School was a struggle of identity—a constant battle of "Can I be popular?" and "Will I ever fit in?" I often found myself sitting alone at lunch, contemplating the meaning of life as I silently ate, waiting for the moment when I could go back to class and be, until the next break in the schedule, in my element.

My friends were few, but I had one lifeline—a friendship with Chuck Donohue. (Incidentally, he's now serving a lengthy sentence in prison for reasons that escape me.) At the time, though, he was my ticket to social survival. When you're gay (whether you've admitted it to yourself or not) and trying to navigate the treacherous waters of adolescence, survival instinct kicks in. I figured, at a certain point, *I may not be on the football team, but I'm smart. Why not use my brains to protect myself?*

So, I became Chuck's tutor, and in exchange, he provided the kind of protection that only a future felon could offer. Suddenly, I was untouchable. The bullies, who had previously targeted me like a pack of wolves on a particularly vulnerable sheep, now avoided me. I was Chuck Donohue's friend, and that came with a certain cachet, or so I thought.

I thought my whole life was about to change when a new girl moved to town—Sue Ellen Cramer. She was the quintessential popular girl, Southern charm wrapped in a pretty package. Everyone adored her, and for a moment, I thought my luck had changed. Chuck pulled me aside one day, his face lit up with the kind of excitement usually reserved for something vaguely criminal. "Hey, Chris," he said, because he couldn't properly pronounce "Christos."

"We're going to play chicken in the field. You, me, Amy and Sue Ellen."

The game of chicken, in case you don't know, was and probably still is the official game of jocks and cool girls: two guys put two girls on their shoulders, and the girls smack each other until someone falls off.

I paused. Me? The geek? Play chicken with them? My heart raced, and not just from the thrill of potential social acceptance.

So there we were, playing chicken, which involved hoisting Sue Ellen onto my shoulders. I was feeling quite proud of myself, balancing her lightly as we tussled with Amy. But then, in a moment I can still conjure up the physical memory of, I felt a sudden warmth trickle down my neck. I looked up, horrified, as Sue Ellen, with the calmness of someone who had just made a very important decision, hissed, "Don't say anything."

She had peed on me.

The realization hit me like a slap in the face. This was what it took to be popular? No thank you. I stumbled off to the bathroom, wiped my neck with paper towels and never spoke to Sue Ellen—or played chicken—again.

On Being "Different"

It's probably time for me to take a break from chronicling my early humiliations and make an important announcement. Are you ready for it?

I'm gay.

I know: I'll let you take a moment to get over this great shock.

At seven, a shirtless Jan Michael Vincent in a Disney movie confirmed what I had suspected—yes, I owe my gay awakening to the House of Mouse, ironic considering I'd go on to work for the very same company. There I was, sitting in the cinema, expecting another fun adventure story, when suddenly I was hit with feelings I couldn't quite name.

The sight of Jan Michael Vincent, tan and muscular, sent a jolt through me that was equal parts thrilling and confusing. I remember getting a stomach ache, my body's physical reaction to the turmoil brewing inside. It was a pivotal moment, one where the vague feelings I'd had before crystallized into something more concrete, even if I didn't have the words to express it yet. These realizations, coupled with my status as the Greek kid in a very un-Greek world, set the stage for years of feeling like an outsider.

In Detroit, I was just another Greek kid in a sea of

Greek kids. In Grosse Pointe, I might as well have been from another planet. But here's the thing about not fitting in—it forces you to create your own space. Every time I felt uncomfortable, every instance of bullying or exclusion, was unknowingly preparing me for a future in which the things that made me me were also my meal ticket.

I learned to find strength in my differences. My Greek heritage, which made me stand out, also gave me a rich cultural background to draw from. The work ethic I learned from my parents, watching them run the restaurant day in and day out, gave me the resilience to persevere through setbacks. And my emerging understanding of my sexuality, while confusing and sometimes frightening, made me convinced I had to get out of my suburban life and see what else the world had to offer.

Adventures in Suburbia, Part II

At least, that's what I say now. At the time, trying to make my way through my awkward teen years as a tall, too-smart-for-his-own-good gay-but-doesn't-quite-know-it kid in Grosse Pointe, I just felt constantly like I was waiting for everyone to point at me and start laughing—probably because sometimes people literally *did* point at me and start laughing.

I did have some spaces in which to be myself, though, and none of them made more of an impact than French class. As an adult, I spend a lot of time in France and I speak French fluently—as someone in the fashion business, a lot of my professional life revolves around what's happening in France, too. As a middle-schooler, all I knew was that France seemed like a glamorous, chic place where I just knew I belonged.

In French class, I found a sense of belonging that had eluded me elsewhere. The classroom buzzed with the energy of new ideas and languages, and for the first time, I felt at home. My teacher, with her passion for Paris and the French language, inspired me. I would often share stories of my Greek heritage and my dreams of visiting Paris one day. In that room, I was not just a student; I was a storyteller, a dreamer. It was a refuge where I could express myself freely, and I cherished every moment spent immersed in the language of love and art.

School outside of French class became a battleground where I expressed my individuality through fashion, despite the jeers and whispers that often followed me. I remember vividly how I would dress up each day, carefully curating outfits that reflected my sense of style. There was something freeing about it, even in the face of bullying. My clothes were armor, a way to assert my identity in a place where I often felt invisible.

Yet, life outside that classroom was a stark contrast. I struggled with the awkwardness of adolescence—my first kiss was a disaster, and social dynamics left me feeling lost. My sister (more on her in a minute) shone brightly in the social scene, while I, the dorky older brother, remained in her shadow, grappling with my own insecurities. I was passionate about music, but I couldn't quite grasp the formula for popularity. Amidst this tumult, though, my Greek heritage provided a sense of community. I had a close-knit group of Greek friends, and the cultural ties we shared were genuinely unbreakable—probably because our parents were all friends and we knew we'd be forced to hang out with each other even if we didn't want to.

It was in Toronto, on a youth trip with my Greek cohort (yes, I was a son of Pericles), where I first decided to embrace my inner punk. I had become obsessed with red leather pants, inspired by the New Romantics of the era. I paired them with a black tie and a crisp white shirt—it was a good look, honestly. Very MTV!

As I walked into the event, surrounded by hundreds of Greek attendees, I felt a rush of adrenaline. But as I strode forward, the laughter and pointing fingers cut deep. In that instant, I became painfully aware of how different I looked. The music seemed to stop, and I felt exposed, vulnerable. Just when I thought I couldn't bear it, two of my girlfriends came to my side, shielding me from the taunts.

Their support gave me strength, reminding me that I was not alone in this fiery moment. I realized then that despite being a conservative kid who excelled in academics, I was capable of stepping into my truth, even if it meant facing ridicule. It was a yin and yang existence, balancing the pressures of fitting in with the desire to stand out.

My Bullshit Detector

My sister, René, is my bullshit detector. I was always the quiet one. The "good" kid. My sister, on the other hand, was...well, she was the opposite.

She was (and still is!) the life of the party, the popular girl everyone wanted to hang out with. She's a year and a half younger than me, but she already had it all figured out, or so it seemed to me. But while I was an awkward loner who couldn't seem to make friends, René walked into classrooms every year only to have teachers instantly compare her to me, assuming she, too, would ace every quiz and constantly have her hand up in the air. She'd roll her eyes and say, "Yeah, I'm Christos's sister, but don't get any ideas. I'm not like him. I'm way cooler."

And she was. She had more friends than I could even count, was on homecoming court, played on the varsity basketball team, and even as a sophomore, she'd show up at senior parties like she owned the place. Meanwhile, I was stuck in my own world, desperate to get an invite to senior parties even when I was an actual senior!

René was smart in ways I wasn't—practical, street-smart and tough. I'd like to think I was clever and capable in a bookish way, but when it came to real-life stuff, like changing a tire or fixing the cable, I was completely lost. And then there was René: always one step ahead, making things happen with her innate common sense and ability to think outside the box.

Which brings us to the story of my first car. I wanted a Ford Mustang, not so much because I thought that was a cool car but because in 1980s Michigan, that's what I thought cool car guys thought cool cars were. What I got was a 1970-something Chrysler Road Runner, licensed by Warner Brothers.

A cartoon car, if you will.

Warner Brothers teamed up with Chrysler, and they slapped Road Runner branding all over the car. It had stripes that made it look like the cartoon character was racing across the side, and the pedals were shaped like the Road Runner's feet. And every time I hit the horn, the car would go, "Meep, meep!"

Can you imagine anything cooler? Didn't think so.

It was like driving a cartoon. But here's the kicker: the car was so bad that if I didn't keep my foot on both the gas and the brake at the same time, it would stall out.

After a while, I gave up on it, because in addition to making cartoon character noises, it also made noises suggesting it wasn't long for this world. I was 16, and I needed a real car—one that didn't require me to babysit it. Once again, I begged my mom for a Ford Mustang. I was a teenager, and the Mustang was the car to have, right? But my mom, ever the realist, just laughed and said, "We don't have money for a Mustang." So, I got the "Virginia Slims" version of the Mustang: a Mercury Capri. It was basically the Mustang's less cool sister—smaller, lighter and decidedly feminine. But it worked, so that was an upgrade.

Now, my mom, in true Greek fashion, wasn't just going to walk into the dealership and swipe a credit card. No, no. She took $5,000 in single dollar bills to the bank one Friday afternoon to get the cash for the car.

She didn't just hand over the money either. She made a big scene, walking up to the teller with the crinkled bills and a look on her face that said: This is how we do things. It was embarrassing and hilarious all at once.

So, I finally had my car, and that meant I could drive my sister to school. We both went to the same high school at that point, and I was trying to be a cool older brother, helping her out. Except for one day, when I came out of class to find my car parked the wrong way, and...the tires had been changed. At first, I didn't think much of it. But then, my sister casually mentioned that one of her friends had noticed the car had a flat and generously offered to fix it. "Oh, that's nice of them," I said, not a clue in the world as to what was really going on.

A few weeks later, my friend Dave Stroyker casually dropped some news into my lap: "Hey, I didn't know your sister was driving your car." I was like, "What do you mean? She doesn't have a license!" Dave just looked at me and said, "Well, I saw her driving it."

My sister, who couldn't even legally drive, had been using my car without asking—or even telling! I was furious. I marched straight to her classroom, caught her as she walked out, and demanded the keys. "Give me the keys to the car!" I snapped. She acted all innocent, like she didn't know what I was talking about, but I wasn't buying it. "You've been driving my car without a license! Give me the keys!"

Looking back, that was just the way she was. Always doing things her own way, always pushing boundaries, always making life a little more interesting. And my mom? She and René were practically inseparable. They both had that classic, no-nonsense Greek woman vibe: spoke their minds and didn't tolerate anyone's bullshit—least of all mine.

Today, René works with me at Covet by Christos, and she's still my bullshit detector and one of my best friends.

And here's an early lesson in manifestation: when the Ford Mustang turned 50 (we are the same age), I was one of the celebrity spokesmen featured in the ad campaign.

Mercury Capri, who?

So Long, Grosse Pointe

All good things, as they say, must come to an end. Things that aren't good, like high school, also come to an end, and as graduation approached, I found myself on the yearbook and graduation committees, planning both our graduation ceremony and my own future.

I was headed to the University of Michigan's main campus in Ann Arbor. Known as a "Public Ivy," it's one of the best universities in the country. My parents were both proud and excited that, as a Michigan native, I'd get in-state tuition. A world-class education at an incredible bargain? What more could a Greek parent want?

As part of our graduation festivities, one of my classmates organized a video where members of our graduating class answered an age-old question:

Where are you going to be in 10 years?

I taped this video and I said, "In 10 years, I'll be working for a major company in international marketing." And I walked away and forgot about it entirely, not because I thought the dream was unrealistic, but because it was so real to me that I had no time to look back—only forward. When I went to my 10-year high school reunion, it was on the eve of my moving to London to work for Disney's marketing department.

They played that video for me, and I won't lie—it felt good to know that, even then, I was putting things out into the universe, trusting my gut and getting to the places I was meant to be.

I also, with *zero irony whatsoever*, convinced everyone that the official theme song of our graduation class should be "I'm Coming Out," which I suppose was also its own kind of manifestation. And yes, I did invite Diana Ross to come speak. Crickets.

Chapter 3

Bonjour, Ann Arbor

After high school graduation, I found myself on a plane headed to Paris. Well, actually, it was to the outskirts of Paris—outside the city, in the beautiful suburbs of France. The family I stayed with were the kindest, most gentle people you could ever meet. They introduced me to the nuances of French culture, from the food to the language to the art of living with a relaxed, *joie de vivre* mentality.

Now, this was a huge cultural shift for me. Grosse Pointe was a place so conservative and segregated that I had never even met a Jewish person in my entire life. The East Side was mainly non-Jewish, the West Side was predominantly Jewish, and then there were a few Greek families scattered in between. But I'd never been exposed to much beyond that bubble. So when I landed in Paris, everything felt new and exciting.

I was struck by how different the world was, and yet

how natural it felt. I remember walking through the streets, taking in the beauty, the language, the energy, and thinking, Oh my God, I'm in, I'm in. I knew this was a city I could live in, a place where I could make a life. It was love at first sight. Paris wasn't just a beautiful city; it felt like home. That trip to Paris was a pivotal one for me.

When I came back to Michigan, I dove right back into my studies, more focused than ever. I was always goal-oriented, and I had big plans. I was attending one of the most competitive schools in the country. The undergraduate business program is tough, designed to weed out those who couldn't cut it. You spent your first two years in liberal arts, then applied to business school for the next two years. It's a rigorous process, and I was all in. I worked my tail off, studied late into the night and did everything I could to get in.

The wait for the admission decision felt endless. This was back in the days before email and instant notifications, so you had to wait by the phone or the mailbox for a letter. Most people would wait patiently, but I'm not most people. Finally, I couldn't take it anymore, so I called the admissions office. I remember getting the nice lady on the phone, and I said, "Listen, I can't wait. Can you please just tell me if I got in or not?" (PS: Such a Gemini move.) She hesitated, but, probably wanting to get rid of me, finally relented and said, "Okay, I'll tell you. You're in."

I almost dropped the phone. There are times in life when you just know something's going to change, and this was one of them. It was one of those defining moments where everything shifts, and I knew that my life was about to take a new direction. Getting into business school was a huge deal. It meant everything to me. From that moment on, I felt like I was on the path to success. I was on fire. My grades were great, I was excelling and I was surrounded by some of the brightest students in the country.

Christos Garkinos, Stylist to the Stars

Things were clicking for me, and even though I was killing it in business school, I still had to hustle on the weekends. No stranger to hard work, I sold my personal football tickets—people take Michigan football really seriously—and also, to make ends meet, I worked at Lord & Taylor, a department store that I absolutely loved.

I sold everything from coats to shoes to scarves, and I did it with a passion. I had no formal retail experience, but I had this instinct for sales that just worked. People would walk in, and I'd be the one to sell them everything —and the salespeople who had been there for years were amazed. It was like they couldn't believe this 20-year-old was out-selling them. They started calling me the "wonder kid" in the sales department.

I was particularly good at the tie department. I had this way of pairing ties with suits, shirts and pocket squares. It was like a game to me. I loved putting together outfits, and the customers could tell. The managers noticed too, but I desperately wanted to move into womenswear and they wouldn't let me—I was trapped in ties! Still, I made the best of it.

One of my proudest moments at Lord & Taylor came

when I put together this killer window display for my favorite brand, Generra. It was beautiful, bold and very much my style. I remember spending hours getting it just right, every detail in place. The moment it was done, I felt like I'd accomplished something truly special—it felt the way I felt when getting a good grade on a paper, but even more me, if that makes sense. And then, something crazy happened.

One day, as I was adjusting my display, I heard a loud, familiar voice behind me: "Excuse me, what's this display? I want it all." I turned around, and there he was —Richard Simmons. Yes, *the* Richard Simmons, the fitness guru and personality. I couldn't believe it. I was in Ann Arbor, Michigan, and Richard Simmons was standing in front of my window display. What was he even doing there? He looked at me and said, "I want it all."

Apparently, he was a fan of the display and wanted to buy everything I'd put together. It was a surreal experience, but it also made me realize something: I was good at what I did. I had an eye for design, for selling, for creating experiences that people loved. I guess you could say Richard was my first celebrity styling client! I ran into him years later, and, wonderfully kind man that he was, he acted as though he remembered exactly who I was.

Saying Oui

At this point in my life, I wasn't out publicly, and if I'm being honest, I wasn't truly out to myself. At 20, I had the incredible opportunity to study in Paris. This time, I felt open to the possibilities of Paris, and as I wandered the streets, I had an unshakable feeling that, for maybe the first time in my entire life, I was exactly where I was supposed to be.

I moved into a tiny apartment in the fourth *arrondissement*, home to the Bastille and a stretch of the Seine where you could walk every evening and watch the sun set behind Notre Dame. I remember setting up my bedroom with care, which involved putting a large photo of my Greek girlfriend—an 8x11 glossy print, like she was an actress and this was her headshot—on my nightstand. I guess I thought this was what boyfriends did.

My roommates were two gay guys. All of us were students living outside of Paris, trying to fumble our way through French life as clueless American teenagers. I hadn't been doing much in the romance department yet —maybe kissed a girl here or there, and I definitely had zero experience with guys.

During the day, I attended a private business school and immersed myself in French culture, learning to speak the language like I'd been born to it and admiring couture in shop windows and eating baguettes. I was the star of my own little romantic Godard film! But by night, things took a different turn. My friends and I were practically broke, so our nights out were often centered around partying as cheaply as possible.

One fateful night, I followed my friends into a gay bar —the first one I ever visited. As the night unfolded, I danced in front of a mirror as the song "High Energy" by Evelyn Thomas blasted through the speakers. I felt, without exaggeration, that this was what I had been searching for. This city, this bar, this moment—I was becoming myself, and that included coming out to myself. By the time I packed up my Parisian bedroom, the 8x11 of my girlfriend was gone.

Once I got back to Michigan, I knew things were changing—I knew I was changing. One Monday night, I met a friend at The Nectarine Ballroom in Ann Arbor, Michigan. The bar had an Alternative Night on Mondays and Gay Night on Tuesdays. My friend and I were there for Alternative Night, as we usually were, and I caught sight of myself in the mirror above the bar while Grace Jones was playing on the screen. I knew: it was time to say out loud, to another person, something that had been true for a long time. I took a deep breath, turned to my friend and said, "I have to tell you something. I'm gay."

She laughed and said, "Duh."

The next night, I was back at the bar for Gay Night, and it was off to the races. Well, the gay races.

The Golden Gate Question

After college ended, I was invited out to California to interview with Clorox—it was one of many interviews I had set up, but it was the only one on the West Coast. I figured, at the very least, it would be a good opportunity to visit with an old girlfriend (the visit pretty much confirmed what I already knew—that I was gay).

They put me up in this fancy hotel...and I mean *fancy*. I felt like I was in a sexy James Bond-style lair. Views of glittering San Francisco stretched out before me like a postcard I could jump into. But this was 1986—and I was terrified. Absolutely terrified. The whole city was wrapped up in an overwhelming fear of AIDS, and I was scared out of my mind. I didn't even dare step into the Castro district because, in my wildly inaccurate 22-year-old brain, I thought maybe I could catch it just by walking around. The energy was electric, but it came with this undercurrent of real danger that I didn't fully understand and yet couldn't ignore.

Clorox was, let me tell you, competitive. The rooms were filled with future Captains of America, and about two of them, myself included, weren't MBA graduates. All the others? Harvard, Wharton, Chicago Business School —all those big-name B-schools dominated the room.

But put me in an interview? Let me talk? Oh, I was golden. I started throwing out stories—memories of growing up helping out in my parents' restaurant. I wove this whole narrative about why I'd be perfect to market their products, craft corporate strategy and soak up business lessons from CEOs, and I must have been impressing them because I kept seeing these slight nods and smirks in return. It felt like the room was rooting for me, the scrappy Greek kid from Michigan, to show all those Wharton WASPs that they had some serious competition.

I finished up my eight (yes, eight!) interviews that day, and the woman sponsoring my visit said, "Come with me." She took me up to the 40th floor of Clorox's building, into a dark conference room where she pressed a button. All of a sudden, these drapes pulled back, revealing a floor-to-ceiling cinematic view of San Francisco, a complete orchestra-playing-in-my-head type of moment. As I caught my breath, I looked over at her and noticed she was grinning at me.

"Christos, we never do this, but we're offering you the job. Today."

Ex-*cuse* me?

Let me tell you, I went from staring at the skyline, starry-eyed, to, "Wait, they want me? Today?" They were offering me a whopping $29,000 (in 1986, I was rich baby, lol) to work on their biggest brand, Kingsford Charcoal. Charcoal! What did I know about barbecuing? At that point, nothing, but I was and am a fast learner, and to this day, I can smoke the hell out of a brisket.

Between the big decision to make and the clarity that, okay, I was actually gay, moving to San Francisco was officially the life-changing fork in the road. The whole what-do-I-do-with-my-life movie moment that I'd end up reflecting on for decades to come.

I called the one person I could think of to call: my mom. "I've got this great job offer in San Francisco, but there's one in Chicago too..." I actually had eight job offers in total, and the one in Chicago—at a top-tier advertising firm—would have been perfect for me. I connected with the more creative types, but I left my heart in San Francisco. So moving there was about something more than work—it was about taking a chance on myself and, as I've continued to do over the entire course of my working life, believing that I was going to be where I was supposed to be. A major pivot.

My mom and I talked it through. And my gut? My gut

was screaming at me pretty loudly, so I took the plunge and said yes to San Francisco.

The Man in the Seersucker Suit

Not that the transition was perfect. The first day of work, I showed up in a seersucker suit, looking pretty chic—or so I thought, at least. The suit was from Lord & Taylor, and it was perfect. Polished, professional and, to my surprise, apparently not perfect at all for corporate Clorox. I got sent home on day one for looking "non-corporate." That hurt, but the next day, I came back in a full-on gray three-piece suit. We adjust.

When I started working at Clorox, something shifted in me—I'd always been a hard worker, but suddenly I was becoming...my father. He was a workaholic, and so was I. I worked incessantly, throwing myself into the grind, spending weekends at the office when no one else was there.

My friends called me a yuppie, and honestly, they weren't wrong. I had this relentless drive to prove something, mostly to myself. At Clorox, I was surrounded by Harvard MBAs and incredibly accomplished people, and I constantly felt like I didn't belong. To compensate, I worked twice as hard. This earned me the reputation of being the "hardworking Greek guy," just like my dad. Looking back, I can see how this intense need to prove myself fueled my quest at overachievement and shaped how I approached everything.

I started as a brand assistant on Kingsford Charcoal, which was Clorox's largest non-home product brand—it was a $200 million business. My role involved everything from crunching budget numbers to coordinating advertising shoots. I was meticulous to a fault. I still remember a barbecue shoot where the actress wasn't wearing a wedding ring. That small detail nagged at me until I demanded they find her a ring. The ad agency hated me for being so exacting, but I didn't care—I was "the Wonder Kid." I had built my identity around being the best and proving myself worthy.

Every morning, I commuted to work by bus, then BART, then walked to the office. I didn't even own a car until a year into the job. The grind was unrelenting, but it mirrored a pattern in my life. I had never missed a day of school for 13 years, never been late, never called in sick. Even as a kid, I was terrified of missing anything or falling behind. That work ethic carried into my career—almost to a fault.

Almost.

One day in 1989, something broke through my rigid routine. MTV was premiering Madonna's "Vogue" music video at 3 pm, and I couldn't miss it. It was going to be an event, and I needed to be there, watching along with every other Madonna super-fan in America.

I made an excuse to leave work early. I drove home just to watch the debut. That moment of indulgence felt monumental, like a rare allowance I granted myself. It also wasn't the last time my Madonna obsession took over my rational brain—more on that a little later in the story.

Figuring It Out

San Francisco was where I found myself—for better and worse. James, my only relationship there, was the best thing that happened to me during that time. We met through a mutual friend, and he was this cute guy working at Neiman Marcus in the pastry section.

I fell hard, and we were together for seven incredible years. Safe, monogamous, loving—it was a lifeline during those years when the world felt so unsafe. Everyone around me in the older generation was getting sick, and here was this man who wanted to stay home with me. He grounded me, and I will always look back on my time with him fondly.

Professionally, San Francisco was where I proved to myself I could do it. I ended up excelling at the Clorox job, knowing nothing about charcoal but working my way into success regardless.

The competition was cutthroat in my class at Clorox, where new hires were constantly being sorted into "tracks," hoping to get moved to bigger and more prestigious teams and, eventually, to jobs higher up in the organization. Being one of the first few people to get promoted in my class felt like a major victory in such a competitive environment. I still remember the heat of the competition—my roommate, a Harvard physics undergrad with a Wharton MBA (basically a genius), didn't get promoted the same day I did. It wasn't a fun evening at home, let me say that!

But more than anything, San Francisco was about survival. It was about thriving, too, but mostly it was trying to stay safe in a world that felt like the wild west. Working, dating, making dumb decisions and learning from them. And in between all that?

Fun. Life.

I went to bars, drank way too much, saw epic concerts—I watched Chris Isaak perform for a crowd of about 100 people.

It wasn't all perfect, obviously. It was, in some ways, a really chaotic period of my life, where I was trying to seem like someone who had it all together while wondering to myself how exactly I was supposed to be the person I wanted to be. San Francisco gave me the space to figure out what the hell I was doing, professionally and personally. I look back and think: thank god I said yes to that move. Thank god I leaned on my gut feeling.

Coming Out...For Good

My sister will deny this story, but it's true! And this is my book, so I'm telling it.

I called René one day and said, "I'm coming home. I've been living with my boyfriend James for two years. René, I'm 24. I need to come home and tell mom I'm gay. I'm pretty much out to my friends here and work. I have to come home and tell her."

René, who still lived in Michigan, was not a fan of this idea. It wasn't that she didn't support me, it's that she didn't want to deal with our mother. I understood what my sister was saying, but I had to do it!

René's brilliant idea was to beat me to the punch.

She thought it'd be cute to walk downstairs after my phone call with her and tell Bessie, "By the way, your son is coming home to tell you something. So I'm going to tell him for you. He's gay."

My mom was gobsmacked. She had no clue! I'd come home for holidays and big Greek dinners and she'd eagerly ask me when I was going to bring home a new girlfriend, and here was my sister telling her there was never going to be a new girlfriend.

In typical understated Greek mother fashion, she looked at my sister and started wailing and crying and banging her head on the washing machine. Literally self-flagellating: she banged her head on the washing machine so hard that she had "Maytag" embossed on her forehead.

After she was finished crying (for now), she called me, frantically, begging me to say it wasn't true.

"Just say you'll try."

I somehow ended the call by telling her maybe I was bisexual, and for the next six months, we didn't really talk.

In time, we got through it. My mother loved her children so much—me being gay was a shock, sure, but it wasn't going to stop her from loving me. She also ended up loving my first husband, Brett, and when we considered adopting children, she threw herself into the idea of becoming a grandmother. Small moments, like watching Ellen DeGeneres come out and live life as an openly gay woman on television, became her window into understanding. She was proud of me, and I was proud of her.

Losing a Titan

My dad wasn't exactly the warm, emotionally available type. He liked to drink and he liked to smoke, and while he tried his best, he was often distant. I remember turning seven: I had this big party planned, but my dad didn't show up. He didn't come home until late that night, and I was worried about him, not knowing where he was or what had happened. Later, I found out he'd been in a car accident. The car had overturned, and he'd been robbed, losing his treasured rings and all the cash in his wallet.

He came to my birthday party the next day, and there's this picture of him in a sling, manning the barbecue in the backyard. It didn't entirely add up for me, but as I got older, I learned some things about my dad I hadn't known as a kid. Apparently, my dad had some ties to the Greek mafia—at least, that's what I was told. He might've had a little gambling thing going on, too, and he was, as I am, more than a little addicted to work.

By the time I was 24 years old—we call 24-year-olds kids today—I was financially responsible for my family. Nick the Greek took care of so many things and so many people but he didn't take care of himself, and at age 58, he was diagnosed with a quickly-moving cancer. A year later, he was gone. Losing him was something that would impact my life for decades to come in ways I couldn't, at the time, even begin to understand. A year earlier, I'd experienced the passing of a close friend, and these back-to-back goodbyes stayed buried as I insisted I was fine to the world and to myself. I threw myself into work, partly because it was an escape and partly because I had no other choice.

The restaurant they'd owned had gone under, and we were barely scraping by. My mom had to sell the restaurant for just $5,000 and we had the house, thankfully, but there was no cushion, no savings to fall back on. I was paying for my dad's medicine when he got sick—at 24 years old.

Looking back, I realize the word that best describes how I felt was anger. I was so angry that he was dying so young and that the responsibility for the family fell on me. He ended up penniless in the end, and that left a real mark on me. It drove my fear—this deep, lingering fear—that I'd follow in his footsteps. While I've always been proud to be like my father in some ways, I couldn't shake the worry that I'd end up like him in the end: penniless and ill. I saw it happen, and it stayed with me.

When I finally reached and then surpassed his age of 59, it was a huge milestone. It marked a turning point in how I saw my own life and my future. But even before then, his situation had already set something in motion for me. I constantly worried—would we lose our house? Would my mom be okay? Would my sister be okay? I'd be lying if I said I still didn't worry about these things. On some level, I probably always will.

That was when the pattern began: me taking care of everyone else. It started when I was so young, and it shaped so much of who I became.

After that, my mom had to make ends meet however she could. She became a nanny, raising other people's kids to support herself. She kept going for the next 25 years of her life, and I did everything I could to help her. I supported her in any way I could—emotionally and financially.

She, in her own way, supported me, too. My mom was old school, though. A lot of things didn't come easy for her, and for a long time, she didn't understand me. I was 23 years old, and I had a big presentation coming up at Clorox. It was my first major corporate presentation, and I was nervous, so I called my mom for support, hoping for some words of wisdom.

Those words?

I'll never forget the way she said to me in her smoker's voice, "Remember. *Nobody* fucks with a Garkinos."

Heartwarming, right? That's Bessie for you.

Turning Down the Ivy League

I had an undergraduate degree from the University of Michigan, and after a few years of corporate life, I felt like it was time to get an MBA. Just any MBA wouldn't do: I had my sights set on Harvard Business School, and I got in.

I had not-so-distant ancestors who couldn't read, and I had a father whose dreams of a big life were beginning to end in Michigan, but I was going to Harvard. The best school in the country, and maybe in the world.

I should have been excited. But in the pit of my stomach, something wasn't right. It's not just that going to Harvard costs a ton of money, which it does. It also, at that point, would have required willingness to shove myself back into the closet (it was 1990 and still I couldn't be out there) and make peace with a certain kind of world that I wasn't particularly interested in embracing. I had already done so much for myself, and I wasn't ready to give it up in exchange for a fancy diploma and a big job. So, with that chapter firmly closed, I started thinking about what would come next, because I knew it was going to be good. It had to be.

The answer came courtesy of my old boss at Clorox, who had left the company and landed a high-up gig at Disney. One day, out of the blue, I got a call from her, dangling the ultimate carrot in front of me: an opportunity to work for him at Disney. Not just in any department—this was the department that oversaw everything from movie soundtracks to theme park music, the kinds of songs that make you feel like you're walking through some kind of enchanted dream world. I'd spent my whole life knee-deep in records, obsessed with the magic of entertainment and driven by the desire to be part of something truly big—here it was.

I packed up my life in San Francisco and jumped into my trusty Nissan Sentra. I drove south on I-5 toward Los Angeles, my head full of dreams and possibilities. LA had no idea what was coming—and neither did I.

Chapter 4

I arrived in LA on August 6, 1990.

Was I ready for Hollywood? Was Hollywood ready for me? Suffice to say, neither of us have been the same since.

Let me paint a picture:

One very well-worn Nissan Sentra SE. It had seen better days, but it did the job of getting me down the coast.

A very unhappy, sweaty cat. The poor thing was wedged in the backseat in a carrier, utterly convinced that I had made a terrible life choice.

A cassette player blaring Madonna's greatest hits—or maybe it was Jody Watley? The details are a little fuzzy now, but a pop diva was definitely the soundtrack of the summer. I was humming along to tunes that made me feel like I was part of something bigger, even though I had no idea what I was doing.

At one point between cassettes, I switched on the radio to hear President George Bush Sr.'s calm but unnervingly stoic voice, announcing the invasion of Kuwait. So, yeah—nothing screams "fresh start" like driving into your new life with the country at war in the background. For me, and for the world, the '90s had officially begun.

Christos Meets the Mouse

I started out, like so many LA newcomers do, as a humble Valley boy, living in a modest little apartment in Toluca Lake, but the thing about living in almost any part of LA is that it really does feel full of Hollywood magic. Was that Robert Downey, Jr. at the next table in a trendy bistro on a Saturday night? Is this person in line behind me at the grocery store an Oscar winner? Is it true that every movie star looks shorter in person?

It was a heady time, full of moments when I felt like anything was possible, especially since I was working at what was arguably the most powerful company in town.

Disney in the '90s? It was on another level. The company was going through a creative renaissance, a golden age of animated films. *The Little Mermaid* was a massive success, *Beauty and the Beast* was shattering expectations, and *The Lion King* was just around the corner, poised to change everything. You couldn't walk into a store or turn on the TV without seeing Mickey Mouse's iconic face, and I was part of the well-oiled machine making it happen.

Some days, it felt like I had wandered into the magical realm of Walt Disney's imagination—except instead of talking teacups and friendly animals, you had power players with egos as big as the Magic Kingdom itself—and, of course, the skills to back those egos up. And instead of a fairy godmother, I had to figure out the rules on my own, which, as you can guess, involved a whole lot of trial, error and bold moves. It didn't take long for me to figure out the lay of the land.

The Pitch

This brings me to one of my most valuable lessons, in business and in life: always, always be ready to pitch yourself—and I really do mean always. You never know when you'll run into someone who could change your life, and when you do, you'd better be ready.

Case in point: my life-changing encounter with Paul Pressler, a half-Greek Disney marketing hotshot. Paul was the real deal—a blend of boardroom brilliance and charm that could make even the most cynical person believe in the magic of Disney all over again. He had a way of making you feel like you were the most important person in the room, and let me tell you, I was all in.

My big meeting with Paul didn't happen in a conference room, or even in an office hallway. It happened in New York City, on the Upper East Side, in the kind of hotel that practically oozes luxury. It was early—like, still-dark-outside early. I was sneaking out for a coffee after a rendezvous with an ex, and after a late night, I was hardly meeting-ready. But as I stepped onto the elevator, there was Paul, and I was left with a choice.

Most people in my shoes would've mumbled some awkward "good morning" and scurried away, hoping to melt into the floor. But I believed then, as I believe now, that what's meant to be is meant to be, and the universe didn't put me in that elevator with Paul by accident. This was a guy you had to book time with months in advance, and here he was—a captive audience!

"So, Paul," I said after we'd said our hellos, trying to act like I always strolled around five-star hotels at dawn looking like I hadn't slept in a week, "just FYI, I speak French. So, you know, if there's ever an opening in Europe..."

Worst case, he'd smile awkwardly, walk away as soon as the elevator dinged and we'd never speak of it again. But...would that really be so bad? It's not like I'd never been embarrassed before. And after all, I knew Disney had huge operations in Europe, and someone had to be working there.

Why not me?

From LA to London: The Great Disney Migration

Fast forward about two months, and I get a call.

It's Paul.

And he's got news. *Big* news.

"We want you to meet with Steve Burke," he says. Now, for those of you not well-versed in the corporate legends of the '90s, Steve Burke was practically royalty in the Disney world. At maybe the ripe age of 32, this guy was already a living legend, a crown prince of the Disney empire, destined for greatness. To even meet him was a big deal. To have him both know my name and want to talk with me specifically was a real business-world coup. Next thing I knew, I was being offered the chance to be Disney's "guy on the ground" for their massive European store expansion.

It was like a fairytale, only better. I didn't have to shove my foot into a glass slipper or fight off a dragon—I just had to sit through a whole lot of business meetings and head off for the brand-new life awaiting me across the Atlantic.

At 28 years old, I boarded a plane to London, and 12 hours later, I landed with wide eyes and a hint of culture shock. First things first: I needed a place to live. Enter my new roommate, Kathleen Turner—no, not that Kathleen Turner (I swear, I looked). We set up shop in Belsize Park, and suddenly I found myself navigating the labyrinth of the London Tube, throwing back cups of hot tea between meetings and working day and night to turn the Disney Store into a shopping destination that rivaled Harrods. I was building Disney's retail empire, brick by magical brick, across the European continent.

The goal, for Disney, was that any child could walk into a store, and without even trying, find themselves in a world where the ordinary became extraordinary. Who wouldn't want to be part of that? This wasn't just about selling products; it was about selling dreams, creating experiences and playing the role of magician, architect and entrepreneur all in one.

No pressure, right?

The Birmingham Blowout

Like any grand adventure, there were challenges along the way, and my first real test was Birmingham. Now, I don't know if you've ever been to Birmingham, England, but it's very different from London—the accent is thicker, the weather is colder and the people aren't afraid to tell you what they think. So when the decision came to open the first Disney Store in that city, I had to get creative. I had to think outside the magic box. And that's when I made it my personal mission to make Birmingham the happiest place this side of EPCOT.

I wasn't about to let the lack of sparkling fairy dust or a castle keep me from transforming the place. I pulled out all the stops. I'm talking about a whole slew of characters, live music and a general air of magic that would make any Fairy Godmother proud. I brought, to this gray, chilly, coal mining-town, a level of enthusiasm that could have lit up an entire city block. The people of Birmingham, I decided, were going to experience the magic of Disney—whether they wanted to or not.

And you know what?

They did.

Ten thousand people lined the streets of Birmingham on opening day. Ten thousand! And let me tell you, they weren't just there to look at the spectacle I'd created, though they certainly loved it—they were there to shop. It was like I had single-handedly turned Birmingham into a temporary Disney wonderland, with Mickey Mouse at the helm. People were lining up for the magic that had gone from my head to the real life streets in front of us. I was literally on cloud nine, high-fiving strangers, exchanging cheers with parents who had brought their kids to the store, and basking in the glow of corporate success.

If this was what it felt like to be Walt Disney, sign me up for a spot in that cryogenic freezing chamber, because I was ready to live forever in that moment. But for now, I was going to enjoy every second of it—at least, until it was time to open the next store.

The Man Behind the Magic

Here's a takeaway from this era of my life: behind every magic moment, there's a tall, stressed-out Greek guy trying to make sure the mayor of a major European capitol doesn't accidentally commit a faux pas that would get said Greek guy fired.

As part of my job supervising the expansion of the Disney Store into Europe, I was in Madrid, where I found myself orchestrating a grand meet-and-greet between Mickey, Minnie and the city's mayor. The streets were packed with thousands of eager Disney fans, their faces lit up with excitement as Mickey and Minnie waved from an open-air convertible. I was in the front, making sure everything went smoothly as we shepherded the world's most famous mice down the streets of Spain's biggest city.

But then, I saw it: an unmistakable disaster in the making. The mayor, who was supposed to be our guest of honor, was holding two plush Mickey and Minnie dolls.

Cute, right?

Wrong!

You see, Disney had an iron-clad rule: no costume characters were ever to be seen handling or interacting with merchandise. Disney magic wasn't about selling; it was about, well, magic. To see beloved characters cast into the role of salespeople would cheapen the brand. They wanted little kids to remember how special it was to meet these characters they watched on TV and at the movies every week. They did not want to have these characters telling kids to buy stuff. It would have been a bad look! For my purposes, it was a cardinal sin that could cost me my job.

Without thinking, I sprang into action. I launched myself through the air, aiming to intercept the mayor before he made the handoff. I remember the moment perfectly—my arms flailing as I collided with the mayor, sending the plush dolls soaring into the air. It's very possible his security thought I was trying to attack him, and in retrospect, I'm lucky I didn't get tackled by a dozen security guards—though if I had still managed to knock Mickey and Minnie out of his hands, it would have been worth it.

On we went to Frankfurt, where once more, Mickey and Minnie were going to appear and delight thousands of fans. The characters were supposed to wear their iconic costumes—suspenders for Mickey and a bright-red polka dot dress for Minnie—but, of course, there was a wrinkle. Someone back at HQ had forgotten to send the crucial black under-skin for Mickey and Minnie. Mickey and Minnie couldn't have bare arms! This was about to be a decidedly un-magical moment. Once more, my corporate survival instincts kicked in.

I dashed through an upscale mall in Frankfurt, finally spotting two (seemingly chic!) bodysuits in a store window. I didn't know the store or the brand, and at that moment, I probably couldn't have even told you where I was, but I whipped out my corporate credit card. I practically flew out of the store, barely pausing to sign the receipt. I rushed back to the event and got the bodysuits onto the characters, then got them out onto the streets. I took a moment to congratulate myself: Christos, I thought, you really nailed this one!

Later, my boss beckoned me into his office. Sitting across from him, I waited eagerly for my next assignment.

"Christos," he said with a quizzical look on his face. "I have some questions about your corporate credit card statement." I looked just as confused as he did at that moment, because I was scrupulously scrupulous when it came to the corporate card. No funny business on my watch! When I asked him to elaborate, he continued. "Why is there a $2,500 charge from Dolce & Gabbana on your statement?"

In my haste to make sure Mickey and Minnie were property attired, I'd somehow managed to spend $2,500 on two plain black bodysuits from one of Italy's most famous—and most expensive—brands.

So there you have my list of early celebrity styling clients: Mickey, Minnie and Richard Simmons.

Parisian Nights and Champs-Élysées Lights

Opening a Disney Store on the Champs-Élysées wasn't just another retail launch. This was, in every sense of the word, a diplomatic mission. You see, EuroDisney (now known as Disneyland Paris) had recently opened, and it needed a boost. The French weren't exactly buying into the whole "American theme park" concept, and we needed the opening of the Disney Store, on Paris's most famed street, to be nothing short of spectacular to turn that tide. We needed something so big, so dazzling, that it could only be described as "international incident" levels of spectacle. This was going to be a defining moment, not just for Disney, but for my journey with the company.

If I may say so, I completely outdid myself with this one. The street was shut down to make way for a massive parade. Thousands upon thousands of people lined the sidewalks, their faces filled with anticipation. And right in the center of it all? There stood Mickey Mouse, Minnie Mouse and, of course, yours truly. We were about to make history. The energy was electric, and we were going to—literally—light up the City of Lights.

For me, though, this wasn't just about Disney magic—this was about my own family. My mom and sister had flown in from Michigan to witness this monumental moment. It was the first time the three of us had been together since my dad passed away, and it was at an event I planned, in a city that had been a beacon of light and love and culture to me for so many years.

So there I am, standing on the Champs-Élysées,

about to be part of something so monumental, so larger-than-life, and in that very instant, I caught a glimpse of my family in the crowd. It was as if time slowed down, and I felt the weight of everything that had led me to that moment.

The lights dimmed.

The crowd hushed.

The music began to swell, building to a crescendo that matched the excitement in the air.

Mickey and Minnie, those icons of joy and childhood, raised their hands in the air. And then, in a moment that felt as magical as any Disney movie finale, fireworks shot from their fingertips. I'm talking about real fireworks—bursting like shooting stars in the night sky above the Champs-Élysées, lighting up Paris in a stunning display.

The entire street erupted in a blaze of twinkling lights, with "Happy Holidays" spelled out in that signature Disney font, casting an ethereal glow across the city. The crowd went wild and in that instant, I realized: this was what Disney was all about. The magic wasn't just in the products or the characters—it was in the emotions, the connections, the sense of wonder we could create. I turned and yelled to my family, "I love my job!"

I'm not saying I cried, but I'll be honest: If you ever see a picture of a grown man in a suit, standing on the Champs-Élysées, openly sobbing while hugging a five-foot-tall Mickey Mouse, I can neither confirm nor deny that it was me. Let's just say that if you look closely, there might be a tear or two glistening on my face as I basked in the glow of the crowd's joy, the fireworks' sparkle and the overwhelming sense of family and magic that enveloped me. It was a once-in-a-lifetime moment, and I wouldn't trade it for anything.

The Best Worst Date of My Life

After Paris, it was time to pack up all the holiday magic and head back to London—specifically, to Regent Street. Same concept as before, but this time, we had some really big celebrities lined up. Sylvester Stallone and his wife were there, and I was standing next to him, fully decked out in my Walt Disney tie and my Disney pin.

By this point, Disney culture was embedded in my psyche—I was completely immersed, and I could recite my talking points in my sleep. It's me and Sylvester Stallone, and Entertainment Tonight is following him around. At some point, they want someone from Disney to go on camera to speak about the event, and I end up being the guy they choose. They turned the microphone toward me, and the interviewer asked, "Who are you?"

"I'm Christos Garkinos, the head of marketing for Disney Stores Europe," I replied.

They then asked, "So, what was it like meeting Sylvester Stallone?"

And without a hint of irony, I looked straight into the camera and said, "It was a magical Disney moment."

Behind the camera, my friends were all losing it, trying not to laugh and whispering, "Oh my God, he's drunk the Kool-Aid."

As soon as the interview wrapped, I realized they were right, and I thought, I need to get out of here.

Disney had practically consumed my life, and while I did genuinely love working there, I didn't have much creative freedom: at Disney, there were a few things you were allowed to do and a much, much longer list of things you weren't allowed to do.

In some ways, this made working there easy, since your options for any given project were limited to things Disney had already okay-ed. At the same time, it meant some of my work felt repetitive, and I wondered what it might be like to work somewhere a little more rebellious.

The next weekend in London, I found myself on a blind date, and let me tell you—it was a disaster. The kind of date that has you asking yourself, "What am I even doing here?" I desperately wanted to be anywhere else, and I counted the minutes until I could make a polite exit. Eventually, I made my escape saying I didn't feel well and, instead of heading home, I ended up at Virgin Megastore.

I should actually thank this guy for that awful blind date—because it led me somewhere pretty amazing.

Let's back up.

My entire life, record stores were a place I went to feel like myself. While in Paris working on the Disney Store project, my version of "me time" was going down the block to the newly-opened Virgin Megastore in Paris, the sound system blasting everything from hip-hop to pop to alternative bands on the verge of becoming the next big thing.

The signature red and white branding was the ultimate in early-'90s cool, and it was a real beacon for pop culture obsessives like me. Richard Branson was one of the first celebrity billionaires, and he was reshaping what the public's idea of a tycoon was. He made running an empire look fun—a party everyone wanted to be invited to. I would say to my friends all the time that my dream job would be to work for Richard Branson as his head of marketing.

In London, Virgin was my go-to spot. I loved standing at the periodicals rack, flipping through Billboard Magazine to see how the latest records were doing. Growing up, I was that kid who'd listen to Casey Kasem and follow the charts religiously, rooting for my favorite artists to climb up to the top. And Billboard was more than just charts—it was my connection to the music industry. I'd even browse the job listings just for fun.

Billboard is printed in America, so by the time they made it to London they were usually a few weeks out of date. That fateful night, after my terrible date, I opened a four-week-old issue, the only one they had, and there it was, staring right back at me: a job listing for Vice President of Marketing at Virgin Megastores in Los Angeles. My dream job.

I know, right? It's almost unbelievable, except I did very much believe I was going to make it happen.

I might not have known exactly how, or exactly when, but I believed and I received. I worked hard, and I was in the right place at the right time, but the third ingredient of my working at Virgin, I know, was manifestation. I truly manifested this job for myself.

Now, Virgin Megastores had only two locations in the U.S. at that time, and this role was all about building a North American chain. It felt like fate. I'd never have seen that job if it weren't for that disastrous date. So, the very next day, I faxed my resume and confidently told them, "I'm your guy."

I wrote to them about my retail experience, my passion for music—everything. As it turned out, I had to fly back to the States for work with Disney anyway, so I lined up an interview, where they offered me the job on the spot. It was one of those things that was shocking but not surprising—I didn't necessarily expect them to choose me, but I also knew that they would.

It was a dream come true. But now I had to go back to Disney, a company that had plucked me from relative obscurity, invested in me, and was, at the time, priming me for a more significant role in the company. I remember thinking: *How am I going to tell them that I'm planning to leave?* When I finally broke the news, they were incredibly supportive, and even asked, "What can we do to keep you?"

I didn't know what to say, honestly.

Then, the very next day, my manager came back with a proposal. Disney was willing to send me to Harvard Business School, and willing to cover the full two years of tuition, if I'd sign a five-year contract to stay with them afterward. Harvard!

Was I finally going to get there? I was floored. I'd have a prestigious education covered, and this security for years to come. Part of me was tempted—who wouldn't be? I went home that evening to my little flat in London, this tiny place that cost about a thousand bucks a month. (Today, that same flat is worth $3 million, by the way!)

That night, I was restless. I went to Harvey Nichols across the street, because I knew, tucked away on the fifth floor, was something that would comfort me—a section of American junk food. I treated myself to Oreo cookies—my absolute weakness—and sat there, munching on them one sleeve at a time, just thinking.

I'm a big believer in trusting my gut, and something in me felt unsettled. As incredible as the Harvard offer was, something didn't feel right. My gut was telling me that this Virgin Megastore job was what I was supposed to be doing. The next day, feeling slightly ill from all those Oreos, I walked into work, thanked Disney for the amazing offer and told them I had to follow my dream.

It was terrifying, turning down a guaranteed future and a life I could easily see for myself, but it was the right choice for me.

I'm maybe the one person on earth who has turned down Harvard Business School twice—but never say never!

I left Disney, moved to Los Angeles and started with Virgin in October 1994. That was the beginning of my career in the music industry. Looking back, I think about how easily life could've gone the other way. I might still be working at Disney, but that one blind date changed everything. Sometimes, life just gives you these moments and you have to trust yourself enough to go after them.

And if you're not sure?

Try eating some Oreos.

Chapter 5

I'm going to say it out loud: in the mid-'90s, I was living a life a million ambitious kids would kill for.

I was the head of marketing for Virgin, which was one of the hottest jobs in Los Angeles. My job was to market the stores, run events and schmooze, especially when it was time to open a new store, which we were doing all the time. I was tasked with turning each opening into its own Coachella-before-there-was-Coachella, and I hit the ground running. Major music labels came to me to run all the advertising and promotions, which meant working on artist relationships and managing deals—not for Virgin Records itself, but for all the other labels, since we were the retailer. It was a huge responsibility.

Virgin wasn't just a company—it was a lifestyle. It was a place where business and creativity collided, and that was something that excited me like nothing else. It was the kind of place where you could wear a leather jacket and actually mean it—where the idea of "going against the grain" wasn't just a slogan but a way of life. For someone like me, who had always been attracted to people and places and ideas that stood out, that broke the mold, Virgin was the dream.

Absolutely nothing prepares you for meeting Richard Branson. The man is an absolute force of nature. He walks into a room and it's electric, his blue eyes even twinklier in person than on TV. He brought a sense of adventure to everything we did, and it was contagious.

One minute, he'd be on the phone saying, "Let's open a Megastore on the moon!"

And I'd find myself sitting there, thinking, *Okay, well, what's the market for lunar retail? Who can we get? Would Cher go to the moon? Would NASA make special red spacesuits?* I'd be seriously crunching numbers on lunar real estate before remembering that lunar real estate wasn't actually a thing.

That was the magic of working with Richard. He had this way of making the impossible sound like a challenge rather than an obstacle. Virgin wasn't just about innovation; it was about taking risks—and doing it with style. No one else in business seemed to have that same fearless, boundary-pushing mentality. It wasn't just about making money; it was about making waves. And that's exactly what we did.

So to give you a sense of what it was like, let's dive right into an average day at Virgin.

Into the Fire

The first big promotion I worked on was with KROQ, one of the major rock radio stations in Los Angeles. Adam

Ant, who was huge at the time, was doing an in-store performance at our Virgin Megastore on Sunset Boulevard. This was a big deal—huge. We promoted it like crazy, the way we knew best—loud, high-energy and in-your-face. Coming from Disney, where I learned that the more people, the better, I figured everything would go smoothly, because that was what Disney was all about —things running smoothly.

But when I got to the store, I realized we had a problem. There were thousands of people outside—way more than we had expected. The entire block was teeming with fans, and inside, the store was just as packed. I was walking through the madness thinking, *I did it!*

But then it hit me: the actual store wasn't big enough for all these people.

Right on cue, I found out that the fire marshal had arrived. This guy would turn out to be a key player in one of the most chaotic events of my career, and I'll never forget him because we ended up becoming friendly years later. At the time, though, I was just trying to avoid a disaster.

It turns out that this fire marshal had just recently become the fire inspector for West Hollywood, and fire safety, for him, was personal: his parents had both tragically died in separate fires. So, as you can imagine, this man was not about to let anyone violate safety rules.

I knew from the moment I introduced myself that he was going to shut us down, which meant we were going to face a riot. The crowd outside was already turning restless, and it could have escalated quickly. They were there to see Adam Ant, and they expected to see Adam Ant.

I knew I had to act fast. I had to get Adam Ant on stage to calm the crowd before things got out of control. So, I ran upstairs and found him in the dressing room we'd set up, putting on the last streak of colorful makeup to complete his iconic look. I grabbed him by the scruff of his neck— literally—and told him, "Whatever your real name is, you follow me right now."

I dragged him to the stage, and he started performing. He did two songs, and I figured that would buy us some time and keep the crowd engaged. But of course, the fire marshal wasn't having it. The moment Adam finished, we were shut down.

I thought I'd saved the day by getting Adam to perform, but it was too little, too late, and the punishment wasn't cheap: the fire marshal fined Virgin $500 for every person that exceeded the limit. We were massively over capacity, and the grand total came out to $50,000. This was my first big event at Virgin, and I honestly thought I was going to get fired. It could have been a "first day at work, last day at work" kind of situation.

Luckily, one of the labels involved in the event helped cover the cost, and I wasn't stuck explaining the expense to Richard.

Okay, so maybe this wasn't an average day. It was a crazy one, though, and I knew things were only about to get crazier.

And for the record? Adam Ant's real name is Stuart.

Making Rules, Breaking Rules

My life at Virgin Megastore was a whirlwind. I was seeing concerts four days a week, meeting everyone from Janet Jackson to Maxwell. I was living my dream—meeting the biggest names in music, and the more events I put together, the more my star rose in the industry. I was also spending a lot of time with Richard, who was unlike any other boss I'd ever had. I was able to be fully out at Virgin, and Richard was both supportive of and genuinely interested in my life. He'd ask me about my love life, and if someone in the office had a juicy piece of gossip or a scene report from a hot club, he'd want the full story.

I'll never forget my first show at Virgin: a Dionne Warwick concert. I was sitting next to Mary Wilson of the Supremes, one of my childhood idols. That's how deep I was in it—sitting next to legends, casually making conversation as though I hadn't spent every spare minute listening to her records as a kid, forcing my family to eat KFC just so I could have an album with her picture on it. People were starting to recognize me, and when I would go out, for work and for fun, people actually wanted to talk to me—I was a long way away from the days of living in Grosse Pointe, wishing someone would invite me to a house party.

I had to manage store openings all over the country, putting on an increasingly-elaborate series of events in major cities. One of the biggest projects I worked on was the opening of the Virgin Megastore in Times Square. We were opening the world's largest music store, and it was a massive deal. Everyone wanted in. It was the party of the year, and we had a lineup comprising what felt like every of-the-moment musician of the '90s, plus a handful of living legends. We booked the Fugees the night their massive and genre-changing first album came out, but we also had Liza Minnelli performing. Foo Fighters, Sarah McLachlan—basically every artist you could imagine was there, and the ones who weren't there were desperate to be invited to the next opening.

I was at the center of it all. The event was a weeklong extravaganza with press, performances and music industry elites. Richard was there, of course, and he had a penchant for doing things in a big, ridiculous way. One of the craziest requests he made? He wanted to jump from the top of the 40th floor of the building to kick off the week's press conference.

It was my job to make that happen. Richard loves jumping off a building, and he makes it look effortless—no one ever thinks about the guy making sure he'll land safely!

The night itself turned into one of the most chaotic events I'd ever been a part of.

As we opened the store doors, the crush of people trying to get in was overwhelming. People were shoving each other to get through, hoping to get closer to the stage, and suddenly, someone fell over the store's balcony, hanging on for dear life. The balcony was three stories high—they easily could have died. My heart sank. I thought, "This is it. This is going to be a tragedy, and it's going to be all my fault."

But out of nowhere, a security guard appeared and saved the person. It was one of those moments when you realize how close you were to total disaster. It was a close call, but we managed to pull it off.

Just as I had at Disney, I was able to include my family in some of my events, though a Virgin Megastore opening was less about tugging on the heartstrings and more about blowing the mind. It was all great to my mother, though, because Bessie had a special love for Virgin Megastore's gift bags. They were always filled with fun goodies, and on one occasion, they included bottles of Virgin vodka. Well, my mother found out about the free vodka in the gift bag, and the next thing I knew, my walkie-talkie was crackling, security on the other end.

"Christos, this lady says she's your mother and wants three bottles of vodka."

Of course.

I went outside, and there she was, not-so-patiently waiting for her vodka. I asked, "Mom, what are you doing?" She replied, indignantly, "I'm getting my vodka!"

She never drank it, but that wasn't the point. It was free vodka, and Greek ladies love a high-value free item.

To this day, that vodka is still sitting, unopened, on a shelf in Michigan.

It's Santa, Baby

A few years after the Times Square opening, I was back at it with another huge event, this time in Chicago. Cher's "Believe" had just dropped and was a massive hit, giving her career a whole new life and a whole new range of fans. She was, at 52, the hottest pop star in the world, and we got the label to agree to bring her in for the Chicago store opening.

Cher was really looking forward to meeting Richard Branson, which was the primary reason she agreed to come. It was a big deal for her, so I made sure Richard was set to be a part of the opening, too.

Just as I thought everything was set to go off without a hitch, I got a call from Richard.

Instead of coming to Chicago to meet Cher and open the new store, Richard was going to Morocco to fly above the desert in a hot air balloon.

Of course he was.

The hot air balloon thing actually was on his schedule —after the Chicago opening. Plans changed, though, and before I could even sputter out a "what do you mean, you can't come?" Richard was telling me he had to go.

"Tell Cher I'll see her in Miami for the next opening," he said casually.

I was in a full panic. Cher was coming to Chicago expecting to meet Richard Branson. Who was bailing on her. And on me!

But I've always been able to think on my feet, so I quickly grabbed the red leather Santa suit I had specially made for Richard.

Oh, yeah. I forgot to mention. It was Christmas, and the plan was for Richard to dress up as rock-and-roll Santa, complete with a hat and a full suit made out of leather, and drag queens dressed up as reindeer were going to pull a sleigh holding him and Cher down the center of Michigan Avenue.

I arrived in Chicago and walked into Cher's hotel

room, greeted by a scene of wigs everywhere—would you expect anything else from Cher?

Her manager, Billy, was there, and Cher was flitting around in the background, preparing for the opening. I took a deep breath.

"I've got some good news and some bad news."

"Okay, tell us the bad news first," Billy said, clearly already bracing himself for impact.

"Well, Richard is going up in a hot air balloon, so... he's not coming to the opening,"

There was a long pause.

Cher looked at me, stunned. I could practically hear the gears turning in her head.

"What?" she asked, with a tone of incredulity.

I took another deep breath.

"The good news is...the parade's still happening, and the costume fits me perfectly!"

It was either sink or swim. I put on the red leather Santa suit, threw on the hat and let myself be pulled down Michigan Avenue with Cher, both of us laughing at the sheer spectacle ahead of us. Literally a dream for a young gay boy from Detroit-making small talk with Cher in a fab, bright-red leather suit.

It was a long day, but it wasn't over.

As we were walking into the store to officially open, I looked over and saw my mother in the vestibule of the Virgin Megastore. We—my sister and I—grew up watching The Sonny & Cher Show, and my mom watched it every week right along with us. Cher was a queen in our house, so to see her in person was nothing short of a miracle in my mom's eyes.

"Mom, Cher! Cher, Mom!"

I felt like the best son in the world. Seeing my mom so happy made it all feel worth it. As it turns out, Cher and my mom had something in common: like Bessie, Cher loved free stuff, so we spent an hour together while she picked out DVDs from the store.

Caught Red-Handed

I've crossed paths with a lot of celebrities over the course of my career—people who were already household names, people who would go on to become household names and people who thought they would be household names but were sadly mistaken. I've seen good, I've seen bad and I've seen ugly, but I've also seen a lot of behavior that was just plain weird. Here's one such story—name redacted to protect the not-so-innocent.

At one memorable opening, I got a call from security. One thing about my time at Virgin: I was always getting calls from security!

"Christos, we've got a problem. A celebrity and his team are stealing CDs on the ground floor. You need to come handle this!"

I went down to the floor to investigate, and sure enough, there was an extremely famous, extremely hot male singer and his friends—stuffing CDs into their jackets. I could not believe it.

I pulled him aside as discreetly as I could.

"Dude, what are you doing? I can literally get you anything for free here. You don't need to steal it."

He looked embarrassed, but at least he got to carry his CDs out of the store in a bag instead of in his pants.

Into the Fire, Again

Another near-miss with the fire department happened while I was on vacation in Australia. After being away for two weeks, I decided to stop by the Virgin store on Sunset to check in and see how things were going.

The moment I walked in, I couldn't believe what I was seeing. There was a band called Nashville Pussy playing live—yeah, that's their actual name. They were a country-punk band, and the store was packed with about 100 people there for the show. But here's the kicker: part of their act involved literally blowing fire from their mouths onto the crowd.

In a record store. In the same record store whose opening almost turned into a riot because of crowd safety concerns and a no-nonsense fire marshal. At least then we were just worried about a possible fire—this was an actual fire, in a store full of plastic!

My first thought was, "Oh my God, is this real life?" I was standing there in total disbelief, watching this band shoot fire over the audience, and I just thought, "Nope. Not today."

Without wasting another second, I went straight to the back and unplugged all the equipment. I didn't even hesitate. Actual fire in a record store?

Absolutely not.

You Can Always Go Downtown

One of my favorite openings, hands down, was when we did the Virgin Megastore in Union Square on 14th Street in New York City.

I had this crazy vision: a huge parade through the downtown streets with drag queens, artists and—most importantly—English singer Petula Clark, singing her classic hit "Downtown." I got Petula to come and sing on a double-decker London-style bus with Richard Branson, and we went all over Manhattan, letting the people of New York know that there was a new destination for everything cool.

While I was planning the event and thinking about who else to invite, I got a call from RCA Records, who had a new boy band they wanted to showcase. They were called *NSYNC and the label wanted to know: could they be on the bus with us?

"Sure!" I said. What's the worst that could happen?

But surely you don't think it was only me, Petula, Richard and *NSYNC on the bus.

We also had Lauryn Hill and Marilyn Manson as part of the opening lineup. Lauryn Hill was promoting her groundbreaking album *The Miseducation of Lauryn Hill*, an instant and forever classic. Marilyn Manson was promoting an album too, and he had his own set of...interesting requests.

One that stood out was his request for three "little people" to be with him at all times. This wasn't a metaphor; he wanted literal small people—as in, under four feet tall—as part of his entourage for the event. It was a true test of my event-planning skills, but I pulled it off, or so I thought.

The day before the event, I was on the phone with Marilyn's team, trying to make sure everything was set for the parade.

"We got the little people," I said to his manager.

"How many did you get?"

"We got three, just like you said!"

"He needs seven, actually," his manager said back to me.

As we were having this conversation, I was in an elevator, trying to maintain my composure.

How was I supposed to pull this off in a matter of hours? This was 1998: I couldn't just Google my way out of this problem. I was stuck with nothing but my wits and a sense of urgency that could only come from being deep in the middle of one of the most insane pop culture riders imaginable.

I still don't know how, but I made it work.

*NSYNC, meanwhile, was on the verge of becoming a massive, global phenomenon, but since boy bands weren't exactly my preferred genre of music, I had no idea just how massive they already were. We were going from one place to the next, hopping in and out of cars, running through a schedule that never seemed to end. But here's the thing I noticed: as we were hitting each stop, it wasn't just the usual crowd of Virgin aficionados and music fans—there were these...girls.

Not a lot, maybe 40 of them at each stop, but still. You could feel it in the air—these guys were a big deal.

Then, we hit Broadway.

When we turned that corner, I saw something I will never forget. There were thousands of girls. Thousands of them. Just waiting, screaming desperately for the *NYSYNC guys to look their way. This was all pre-cell phone era, so I was completely unprepared for the magnitude of it all. It was like a Taylor Swift energy before there was even a Taylor Swift.

We were trying to navigate through this sea of screaming fans, and I was thinking: *This is it. This is pop culture history.* I could feel the energy buzzing in the air. It was palpable. It was electric. And then we pulled up, and the boys headed off to meet the crowd while I was standing there trying to manage the madness.

And then—of course—something else happened.

I turned around, and there was Marilyn Manson. He was getting out of a limousine, flanked by the seven little people he insisted were key to his attendance. Richard, standing next to me, looked at me, wide-eyed.

"Christos," he said. "What's up with this guy?"

"I don't know, Richard. I really don't know."

There was Marilyn, strutting around in his leather get-up, while *NSYNC's fans were still screaming in the background. It was like two worlds colliding—the boy band frenzy and the anti-establishment shock rocker energy. The contrast couldn't have been more stark. *NSYNC, the golden boys of pop, surrounded by legions of fans. Marilyn, the prince of darkness, surrounded by his small entourage.

And then Richard, being Richard, pulls out a bottle of champagne. That's his thing: he always sprays champagne at openings, as a way to make everything feel extra-celebratory. As I saw him aim the bottle, I rushed over, catching him just before he popped the cork.

"Richard," I said, "do not spray this bottle in the direction of these *NYSYNC fans. They're all fourteen!"

He didn't: instead, aimed the bottle a little too high, and it hit Marilyn Manson, who was pissed, since he was in head-to-toe leather that was now soaking in champagne.

I could feel the tension, and I figured that would be the moment it all fell apart, but it didn't. We all managed to get through it somehow, heading off to the opening party. The next day, I walked into the store's back room only to discover that someone had stolen all the equipment from the catering team overnight—all the computers, the burners, even the pots and pans.

Another thing at Virgin: you really, truly never know what's going to happen.

Down the Rabbit Hole

It might be an exaggeration to say that after a few years at Virgin, I'd seen it all, but I think it was pretty close.

I'd worked with the Spice Girls and watched Brandy and Monica sing "The Boy Is Mine" for the first time. I rode in an elevator with Ricky Martin, and I was there when Whitney Houston made her big comeback after everything she'd been through.

One night, I was out with my mentor, Ian, a guy I absolutely loved. We were heading to a place called No Bar, a cool if-you-know-you-know kind of spot in New

York. I don't smoke pot, but this night for whatever reason, I did. And I was high as a kite. The whole night felt surreal. We smoked a joint, and I walked into that bar thinking, "I'm the number one guy in town. This is how my life is now."

I went to the bathroom, and standing beside me was the hottest male VJ on MTV at the time—this guy was the object of everyone's fantasies, and here he was, inches away from me in the bathroom of an exclusive club.

I, in all my marijuana-induced glory, thought, "Is this it? Am I about to hook up with this incredibly hot and famous guy in the bathroom?"

He leaned closer.

"Hey, I just want to tell you...you've got some toilet paper stuck to your shoe."

I looked down. Sure enough, there it was.

"Thanks," I mumbled.

Boom—the tetherball, once again, hit me right in the head.

A real night off was a rarity for me, though—I worked so hard, and I was always working, overseeing these multi-million dollar events and also, occasionally, running sensitive errands, like that time I had to go get weed for Jamiroquai.

I booked Jewel her first in-store performance back when she was living out of her car. She quickly went on to become a superstar, and that part of the job meant a lot to me—to not just reflect what was already cool and popular but to look forward, thinking about the future of music and culture.

When I was right, I was really right, but I wasn't right all the time. At one party, I was chatting with the male model and actor Tyrese when someone introduced us to a gorgeous group of young women dressed in coordinated outfits. They were a girl group, and each one told me her name:

"I'm Beyoncé."

"I'm Kelly."

"I'm Latavia."

"I'm LeToya."

They were so sweet, and I asked what their group was called. Beyoncé, the leader, said, "We're called Destiny's Child."

We finished making small talk and moved on, and I turned to Tyrese. *Sotto voce*, I gave him my take.

"They *have* to change the name of this group. They'll never make it otherwise!"

A Full-Circle Scandal

One day, I found myself tasked with opening a store at Downtown Disney, the Disneyland-adjacent outdoor shopping and dining center that has become one of the brand's most popular and most profitable investments.

It felt like a reunion for everyone who was important in my life. Richard was there. My family was there. My ex-coworkers were there.

But here's the kicker: since this was a Virgin event and a Disney event, it was only fitting that we have a slew of Number One artists. And wouldn't it make sense to include a performance of the nation's current Number One song?

The biggest song in America at that time was by a singer-songwriter named Meredith Brooks, and it was called "Bitch."

I was going to produce an event outside the gates of Disneyland and the main attraction was going to be a lady singing the word "bitch" on repeat. Or was I?

Disney did not want Meredith to sing the word "bitch." And they were Disney! It was their way or the highway.

I knew what was going to happen.

There was no way Meredith was going to sing a censored version of that song. What would she even change it to: "I'm a witch"? As in...Ursula from *The Little Mermaid*?

No way.

I called Richard, explained the situation, and said, "What do you think?"

Richard was all in—he didn't care about a little light swearing, and he was my boss. His word was final!

Meredith hit the stage, and the crowd went wild. When she got to the chorus, she screamed, "I'm a bitch!"

It echoed throughout Downtown Disney, and once again, people—many of whom were my former coworkers—started running at me. They were furious, and while I pretended it had been out of my control, I'm hard-pressed to think of a funnier moment from my years as a marketing hotshot.

Like A...Well, You Know

Whenever we opened a new store, we had this thing we'd do. We'd tell the crowds outside, "come on in, it's time to meet us!" And we always queued up a specific song because, well, this company was called Virgin.

The song, of course, was "Like a Virgin," by Madonna. Every time we opened a Virgin Megastore, that song blasted through the speakers as the doors opened. It became a tradition, something everyone expected. People would walk into the store, hear the song and know exactly what was happening. It was like our theme song—our national anthem.

In San Francisco, I had Exene Cervenka, lead singer of the punk band X, on the roof, and we also had secured a big-deal pop star to appear in conjunction with the release of her new album. Looking back, I should've thought a little more carefully about our store opening, but it was tradition. Who questions tradition?

The doors opened, and I said into the mic, "Ladies and gentlemen, here she is!"

"Like A Virgin" starts playing, and I have a slo-mo realization: we have a rival pop diva in the building. The singer, standing backstage, completely lost her shit. I mean, she really lost it.

She screamed, "I can't believe you played that bitch's song!" over and over again. She was furious, and the next thing I knew, she locked herself in her dressing room, refusing to come out. We had hundreds of people in line to meet her, and the whole event was about to fall apart.

I had to go in there, knock on her door and beg

her forgiveness. Seriously, I got on my hands and knees in front of this woman and apologized over and over.

I kept saying, "Listen, it was a mistake. I'm so sorry, please come out. We love you. It was a mistake!"

Finally, she agreed to come out, but we had to play every single one of her songs we could find in the store to make it right.

Looking back, I think part of why I was able to smooth things over was because I have this natural ability to convince people to do things—in a good way! It was the same thing that helped me when I convinced Cher to be a part of something, or when I got other celebrities to come around, or when I was pitching myself in an elevator or in a boardroom filled with executives. It was like this knack for getting people to say yes.

And, believe me, at Virgin? I needed it.

Popping Bottles

One year, I was attending the MTV Music Awards in New York. A friend of mine was Janet Jackson's assistant, and I hadn't met Janet yet, but I knew she'd eventually do an in-store at Virgin, so I was looking forward to it. A few of us—not including Janet herself—were in Janet's hotel room for the pre-party, hanging out and having a good time.

Champagne arrived—good champagne. Someone asked if I wanted some.

Wasn't this Janet's champagne?

"She's not going to drink it," someone told me. "She's a Jehovah's Witness."

I just shrugged and figured that was that, happy to toss back a glass of the good stuff. As I sipped (and sipped some more), it wasn't lost on me that drinking high-end champagne in Janet Jackson's hotel suite was exactly where a younger version of me would have imagined himself on those cold, lonely days on the playground.

Well, we finished the champagne, and then there was a knock on the door.

"Janet's team is asking if the champagne's ready!"

"What? What champagne?!"

I looked around the room and realized the bottle was empty. Since we were at a hotel, my first thought was to call down to room service for a replacement. Quick thinking, right? I called the hotel's front desk and asked if they could send another bottle up to Janet's room.

"Sure, that'll be $1,250."

I almost dropped the phone. There was no way I could afford that! I frantically asked, "Can you send another bottle of champagne but, like, one that doesn't cost $1,250?"

The Spice Girls, one of the hottest groups in the world at that time, were standing there, watching me lose my mind over this champagne situation. I was incredibly stressed out, but I also recognized the absurdity of the moment. In another "wow, I somehow made this work" moment, I secured a new bottle of champagne for Janet, though I don't know whether or not she drank it.

This life wasn't always glamorous, but it was always an adventure.

The Crowd Goes Wild

One day, Richard called me up and said, "Christos, I'm going on *The Tonight Show* with Jay Leno. Want to come with me?"

Richard Branson. Jay Leno. *The Tonight Show.* This was not something I could pass up. We drove over to the studio in my Saab convertible with the top down, me smoking cigarettes, and I had never felt cooler.

Richard and I were hanging out in the dressing room before the show, and the producers came in with the pre-show questions. It's funny—Richard Branson is one of the most famous men in the world and certainly one of the most successful, but he's actually quite shy, especially around and in front of big crowds.

One of the questions they had for him was about billionaires and their obsession with hot air balloons. Billionaires, as you might remember from the Chicago Christmas Cher Extravaganza, are always flying around in balloons, and Jay Leno was going to ask him about it.

Richard was stressed.

"Christos, what do I say to that?"

I said, "Tell him you don't know, but you've been wondering: what is it with millionaires and motorcycles?"

Richard goes on stage, Jay asks the question, and Richard delivered my line perfectly.

The crowd absolutely lost it. They went crazy. Richard nailed it, and it was such a proud moment for me.

Richard Branson, Jay Leno and me—just a Greek kid from Michigan helping a billionaire make a joke about balloons on a national TV program watched by millions of people.

The End of the World As We Knew It

When Napster came along, I was one of the people who didn't think it was going to make much of a difference.

"What's digital music?" I thought. "People say they don't want CDs anymore, but it's just a trend."

I said as much on Fox News when they invited me on, as a representative of Virgin Megastores to opine on the future of media. People loved Virgin Megastores, and they spent money there. I myself had been going to record stores since I was a little kid—that was never going to change.

A year later, I was out of a job.

Working for Virgin changed my life. I met a lot of famous people, sure, but I also learned so much about myself and so much about business. Richard cared so much, not just about profits but about experiences: he'd say to me all the time as we prepared to open new stores, "Christos, I don't care if they buy anything. I care about whether or not they have fun." That's a philosophy I've brought with me in everything I've done since and into everything I'm still doing.

It was an era of fun, but like all eras, it came to an end. It was time, once again, for me to figure out what was next.

Where it all began. Nick the Greek and Aspasia on their wedding day...

Always a fashion plate, circa 1968

As seen and so true at Meat Town Inn—my parents' restaurant

1970's in a picture
with my sister René.
God i want that suit!

My dad Nick the Greek,
always debonair

Disney Days, 1994

The day I saved
my job in Madrid

One word.
Cher.
Chicago Megastore Opening

With Ru-Paul.
My hair almost as poufy

Garcelle and I on the red carpet

My dog Sophie, who saved my life

Campaign shot, Ford Mustang 50th anniversary

Shoot in front of the now closed Meat Town Inn

The launch of Covet by Christos

ChristosCon Greece with #stossquad

#stossquad can't sleep while shopping

Always a Mama's Boy.
Aspasia

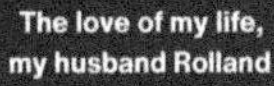

The love of my life,
my husband Rolland

Chapter 6

One moment, you're working at Virgin Megastores, rubbing elbows with music industry icons, surrounded by the buzz of new releases and the thrill of live performances. The next, you're knee-deep in designer resale, dressing celebrities and industry insiders and eventually landing your own TV show.

At Virgin Megastores, I found myself in the heart of a world that many could only dream of. Every day brought a new project, a new artist, a new collaboration. There was a thrill to it—the kind of energy that's hard to explain, but anyone in the industry would know it well. I worked alongside big names, had backstage access and was, for a time, living in a world filled with music and creativity.

After I was laid off, I was offered a position at a high-flying tech startup. It was one of those ventures that seemed destined for success—fast-paced, filled with young talent and driven by innovation. For a time, it felt like I had landed right back into the same fast lane I'd just left in the music industry, albeit with slightly less hot air balloon drama. We burned through $50 million in marketing money in just six months. That's right—$50 million in six months. Every week was a new campaign, a new concept, a new pitch to investors.

This startup burned out—fast.

After six intense months, it all came crashing down, and I found myself jobless. It was disorienting. After living in the heart of two industries filled with so much energy and promise, I was suddenly left with silence, wondering what my next step would be. It was stressful to not be working and stressful to not be making money —I'd been holding down a job (sometimes more than one) since I was a six-year-old cashier at Meat Town.

As the days passed, I began to reflect on my own dreams—things I had put aside while chasing the excitement of music and tech. I didn't want to work for another music company or another startup: I was, you might say, coveting a comeback.

One dream kept coming: getting into fashion. This wasn't a new idea; it was something I'd been fascinated by since childhood. Growing up, I had this memory—almost like a reel in my mind—of watching my dad get dressed every morning. He had a ritual, a real pride in his appearance, and it wasn't just about clothes; it was about elegance, detail and showing the world the person you wanted to be. My dad, the handsomest Greek in all of Michigan, was meticulous, right down to the way he put on his cufflinks.

Those cufflinks fascinated me. They were small, perhaps inconspicuous to others, but to me, they represented a sense of style and care that I wanted to bring to my own life.

As I grew older, those cufflinks lingered in my mind. They held more than just a memory; they held a sense of identity, a connection to something meaningful. Years later, my sister would give them to me on my 60th birthday, a deeply personal gift that brought that early fascination with style full circle.

Maybe in a way, those cufflinks had been quietly guiding me toward my own journey in fashion. With the startup now behind me, I found myself revisiting that old dream with a new sense of purpose.

In 1999, I made my fashion dreams come true when I became an early pioneer of high-end designer resale and celebrity styling. I didn't know when I started that it would put me on a path where I'd be meeting icons like Donatella Versace, dressing celebrities and establishing a name as one of the go-to stylists in the world of designer resale.

One day, sorting through an array of Chanel tweed jackets and slinky YSL cocktail dresses, I heard a voice from behind me. It was distinct and familiar—a low, gravelly accent that carried a tone of authority.

I turned around, ready to politely tell whoever it was that I was busy, when I realized I was standing face-to-face with none other than Donatella Versace. My jaw nearly hit the floor. There she was—*Donatella Versace*.

Somehow I managed to stammer a casual, "Oh hey, Donatella," like I'd been expecting her all day.

How on earth do you turn away Donatella Versace? It felt like one of those bizarre dreams where everything seems almost real but a little surreal. I was starstruck, flustered and more than a little flattered: Donatella Versace wanted *my* styling help.

That brief moment turned into a memory I would carry with me, a sort of "pinch me" moment that marked the beginning of many surreal encounters to come. These types of encounters quickly became commonplace, but that first one stayed with me. It was like the universe was sending a signal: This is your path. Buckle up.

Styling: It's an Art

I became a go-to guy for one-of-a-kind styles, and as I leaned further into this niche, I found myself dressing over 13,000 women, each client bringing their own unique personality and style into the mix. It wasn't just a way for people to buy clothes—it was a way for fashion lovers to connect, to swap stories, to experience the energy and glamor of designer fashion without the pretense. People worked with me not just for the clothes but for the experience, the chance to find something special, something with real personality.

The surprises didn't end with Donatella. My reputation started attracting a unique array of people: actors, musicians, socialites and even everyday people who simply wanted to touch a bit of the magic they'd seen in the world of Hollywood and high fashion. It wasn't unusual for someone to call me looking for a special piece for a once-in-a-lifetime event—a wedding, an anniversary, a reunion. Each client had a story, and they were drawn to the unique, luxurious and often storied items I collected.

What surprised me most was the depth of the connections I made through this work. I never anticipated how meaningful these interactions would become, how a simple purchase could lead to shared memories, laughter and sometimes even tears. I began to see fashion not as a mere business, but as a form of storytelling—each garment a chapter in someone's life, each purchase a chance to rewrite a part of that story. Fashion became the fabric through which people expressed who they were or, sometimes, who they wanted to be.

Moments like the one with Donatella were certainly glamorous, but they were just part of the larger tapestry. What began as a straightforward idea—reselling beautiful things from celebrity closets—had morphed into something richer and more complex than I could have imagined. With every garment, I wasn't just making a sale; I was sharing history, memories and a bit of magic with each client. And through those exchanges, I came to realize that I wasn't just building a business—I was building a legacy, one designer piece at a time.

I also accumulated a lot of crazy, only-in-Hollywood stories. Aren't you curious?

An "Only In LA" Encounter

When you're handling designer pieces for high-profile clients, the job sometimes requires you to navigate situations that are way outside the ordinary. There's one particular experience that still makes me laugh—and blush—a little whenever I think about it.

It all started with a pair of black leather pants and an LA news personality who called me looking for something edgy and iconic. She was known for her on-screen style, and the pants I found and brought to her were exactly what she needed to make a statement. They were sleek, fitted and undeniably bold—a perfect reflection of her persona. But as with any bold fashion piece, these pants came with their own challenges.

As she tried them on, she struggled with the zipper, so I stepped in to help. There I was, kneeling in front of her, carefully wrestling with the zipper that just wouldn't budge. My focus was entirely on the task at hand—until, in one moment of unintended eye contact, I realized something that made my cheeks go red: she wasn't wearing any underwear.

Time seemed to stand still as I froze, trying to process what I'd just seen. My face must have turned several shades of crimson, and for a split second, I didn't know where to look or how to react. But as I tried to regain my composure, I looked up to see that she was completely unfazed. She gave me a casual smile as if this were just another Tuesday.

Meanwhile, my inner monologue was in full panic mode: Stay professional. Don't react. Just focus on the zipper. Somehow, I managed to get through the rest of the fitting without any further incident. I finessed the zipper into place, nodded approvingly and made a few last styling suggestions before she left.

Ten minutes later, I got into my car, still replaying the

awkward encounter in my mind. Driving down one of LA's busiest streets, I came to a stop at a red light and looked up. And there she was—staring down at me from a massive billboard, larger than life. It was the kind of cosmic irony you couldn't make up. One moment, I'd been in her very personal space, and the next, she was towering above me in the LA skyline, looking poised and glamorous.

I'd never watch the news the same way again.

A Model Life

One time, Naomi Campbell reached out to me for help finding something special. She was the sweetest thing ever—seriously! I helped her pick out an incredible piece. As someone who loved fashion and fashion culture, playing dress-up with Naomi Campbell, chatting and watching her try things on, was absolutely surreal.

And then there was Iman—what a force. She's not just a legendary supermodel and businesswoman; she's also an incredibly smart shopper. At our first meeting, she impressed me by immediately asking the question vintage shoppers in-the-know love to ask:

"So, what do you have in the back?"

It was code for "what do you have that you haven't shown anyone else," and it worked.

As it happened, I did have a bunch of stuff I hadn't officially put up for sale yet, and Iman was more than game to sort through it with me—it was like ultra-luxury dumpster diving! It was one of those how-is-this-my-life moments—just me and Iman, elbow-deep in vintage finds.

Over the years, I styled some incredible people. Amal Clooney was a regular client of mine for about six months. I've always admired her timeless style, and working with her was an absolute joy. Then there's Winona Ryder, who remains one of my all-time favorites thanks to her kind nature and innate personal style. Another woman I loved styling—and consider a friend to this day—was Selma Blair. She, too, had a sense of style money couldn't buy, and it was always fun to try the most outlandish couture pieces on her—she was game for anything.

One of the most special moments was styling Emma Stone for her very first Hollywood party. Seeing her career take off after that moment still fills me with pride.

I was left genuinely starstruck when Catherine Deneuve wanted to shop with me. The French actress had actually been personal friends with many of the designers whose creations I sold, and her style had been shaping tastes since the 1960s.

Another moment I'll always look back fondly on was styling the iconoclastic Irish singer Sinead O'Connor. She told me she was attending an amfAR event and said something that really stuck with me: "I want to feel pretty."

This was later in her career, well beyond her "Nothing Compares 2 U" days, and it touched me that after everything she had been through, she trusted me to make her feel special on an important night. I spent a day and a half with her, going back and forth to find the perfect look.

I ended up putting her in a Hervé Léger dress, which might sound surprising—the super-sexy, bombshell brand Hervé Léger on Sinead O'Connor? But it worked. She looked stunning.

That night, as she was heading to the event, she turned to me and said, "Christos, I feel pretty. Thank you so much." Those were her last words to me that evening, and they stayed with me forever.

Behind the Glamour

In fashion, you see a lot of people in vulnerable moments. I had a client call me one day about her wedding dress, and it instantly told me one of two things: either she was in need of money, or she was going through a divorce and no longer wanted the dress. Turns out, it was the second. She was the daughter of a famous musician, and her marriage was ending. She said it was a really sad moment, and I could sense her emotional struggle.

The dress itself was absolutely stunning, though, and even though I didn't usually take wedding dresses on consignment, I decided to make an exception for her.

I had a big pop-up event in New York coming up, and the dress was so beautiful that I couldn't leave it behind. I took it with me on the plane, carefully placing it next to me on the seat since no one else was sitting there. It felt like it deserved its own space. Once we arrived in New York, I put the dress in the window of the pop-up shop.

As fate would have it, a girl was walking by in Soho, and she stopped in her tracks. She looked at the dress and said, “Oh my God, I think that's my wedding dress!” She could just feel it. She tried it on, and it was a perfect fit. The joy on her face was unforgettable.

When I told the original owner what had happened, I was able to describe this beautiful moment—how the dress, which had brought both joy and sadness, had now moved on to someone else, ready to bring them happiness.

That moment really struck me, because it gets to the heart of what I believe I really am—a storyteller. Using one dress, I was able to weave two separate tales together, linking both of these women forever in a way that brought meaning to each one. It’s a skill I would continue to hone, and I think it’s one of my most precious gifts.

The Hoarder

One day, my phone rang. The caller ID flashed “Unknown,” but I answered anyway, my curiosity piqued.

“Hi,” the woman said, her voice both urgent and oddly composed. “I hear you...help people.”

Now I was really curious. Where was this going?

“Yes, I do. How can I assist you?”

There was a brief pause on the line. “So, I have a problem,” she said finally. “I'm a hoarder.”

Visions of cat litter boxes and old cans started to dance through my head, but I stayed on the line.

“I hoard...Chanel.”

She went on to tell me that she had accumulated an astronomical amount of Chanel merchandise. It wasn't just a few bags and shoes—no, it really was a full-scale hoarding situation, and her apartment was overwhelmed with luxury goods. "I need to get rid of it," she said. "I have a problem, and I need help."

I leaned back in my chair, trying to process the enormity of the situation. "All right," I said, attempting to sound as calm as possible. "Where are you located?"

"New York," she answered.

My heart skipped a beat. "I'm in LA right now," I said. "But I can be there tomorrow."

Within 48 hours, I found myself standing on a street in Manhattan, staring up at an imposing building. She directed me to a building adjacent to her own, where her massive collection was stored—this wasn't just her apartment, it was her Chanel apartment. As in, one place was her home, and the other place existed to store Chanel.

When I arrived at the apartment, I knocked on the door and waited. My thoughts raced—what was I going to find behind that door? Finally, the door creaked open, and there she was, looking both relieved and apprehensive.

"Come in," she said, stepping aside. My eyes widened as I took in the sight before me. The hallway was barely visible through the piles of Chanel items that filled the space. It wasn't just a collection; it was an avalanche of fashion. I didn't know whether to cry or orgasm.

As I stepped inside, the sheer volume of the

merchandise took my breath away. There were stacks of boxes, shelves overflowing with bags and garments spilling out everywhere. There were pieces from last season and from two decades ago, and all of it was in perfect condition. I turned to the woman, who seemed both hopeful and defeated.

"Where do we start?" I asked, trying to regain my composure.

"For the next four days, this is your world," she said with a resigned smile.

And so began the marathon of sorting through the Chanel treasure trove. Each day was a whirlwind of activity. I meticulously cataloged every item—I discovered exquisite handbags with intricate detailing, stunning couture dresses that were more works of art than clothing.

My mind boggled at the thought of the total value of this collection. The woman's problem had become my challenge. I had to find buyers for these items, ensuring that each piece found a new home where it would be cherished.

Throughout the four days, we developed a routine. I would sift through the piles, photograph the items and document their details. The woman helped as much as she could, though it was clear the process was emotionally taxing for her. Each item seemed to hold memories and a certain sadness.

By the end of the fourth day, we had managed to make significant progress. I had a stack of consignments ready and a clear plan to reach out to potential buyers.

In the end, I sold the collection on her behalf, and she managed to reclaim a sense of normalcy in her life. The experience was both bizarre and fascinating, and while I'm not sure if she's still hoarding, I certainly hope she'll call me if she develops a weakness for Hermès.

Real Friends

Styling is an intimate business, as you probably figured out reading the story of the nearly-naked news anchor. Women would come into the store and within a matter of minutes, I'd be on my hands and knees, pinning their skirts and offering my most honest opinions about cut, color and date choice.

I'm lucky to say that many of my clients became true-blue friends, none more so than the gorgeous, inimitable model, actress and media mogul Garcelle Beauvais, whom you might recognize from movies like *Coming to America* and TV shows like the ever-popular *Real Housewives of Beverly Hills*.

I'll never forget meeting Garcelle for the first time. Her presence was magnetic, and she had an energy that could fill a room.

She was and is a celebrity who didn't take herself too seriously, and she had real spunk—I knew instantly we were going to be friends. It didn't hurt that she's one of the most beautiful women in the world, and styling her was almost too easy, since she looks incredible in everything.

Garcelle would not only come back to work with me again and again, but she'd become one of my closest friends. We've shared countless laughs, late-night conversations and stories about life in Hollywood. Garcelle has this warmth and humor that make her easy to be around, and she's never lost that down-to-earth quality, even as her fame grew. She's remained a loyal friend even in my hardest moments, and we've had some real fun together, like the time we met one of the most important men in all of fashion.

I went as her date to a Tom Ford sunglasses launch, and I had chosen a double-breasted Fendi suit for the occasion. We walked up the store's grand staircase towards Tom Ford himself. He's a handsome, incredibly-talented designer who breathed new life into Gucci, launched his own spectacular line of clothes, fragrances and sexy shoes, and pivoted into film, where his first efforts were lauded by everyone in Hollywood as Oscar-worthy. I had met Tom on one other brief occasion, but this was a more intimate gathering, and I was certain to get some face time with the man himself.

We were giggly and nervous, like a couple of kids. Naturally, Tom spoke to Garcelle first—after all, she's Garcelle. A celebrity through and through, her aura made her an inevitable first stop.

When my moment came, I introduced myself:

"Hi, Tom. I'm Christos Garkinos. We've met once before. How are you?"

In truth, I wasn't sure he remembered me. His reaction wasn't immediate, and in that pause, I began to overthink.

He doesn't know me, does he?

He stepped back, and my stomach churned

with uncertainty. *Oh my God*, I thought. *What's he going to say?* Then, with deliberate intention, he looked me up and down. My heart skipped. Here it comes—this is either going to be amazing or a disaster.

"Nice suit," he said.

Time seemed to freeze. For Tom Ford—the icon of elegance and impeccable taste—to step back and utter those words? That was it for me. I was stunned, thrilled and utterly validated. In that moment, I knew my night had peaked. "Thank you very much," I thought to myself. "Good night, everybody. End scene. Life is good."

Tom Ford had spoken, and he approved.

Let's Take This Show on the Road

By the late 2000s, I was a bona fide LA personality. Luxury resale was a huge market, and it felt like every day, a fabulous new client was calling, wanting to be styled by me and, oftentimes, wanting to invite me along on nights out. I was used to standing next to celebrity pals as paparazzi snapped away, and I was no stranger to a red carpet.

Still, it wasn't like I was *trying* to jump in front of the camera myself.

Famous last words.

The Christos Garkinos Top 25

I've been working in fashion for a long time—more than 25 years. In honor of hitting that milestone, and since people often ask me for styling secrets, I decided to put together my own version of The Rules, Christos-style.

25. Always go with your gut. This is more than a fashion rule—it's a life rule.

24. Vintage should always look modern.

23. Skinny jeans are, 99 percent of the time, a no.

22. Tom Ford-era Gucci is, 100 percent of the time, a yes.

21. A great black clutch will change your life. I guarantee it.

20. Study Catherine Deneuve and Fran Drescher for style inspiration. Catherine and Fran: they'll always spark an idea.

19. Finding your right bra size will change your life. Ask Oprah.

18. The color green. That's it. Green!

17. Another brand worth collecting? Dries Van Noten.

16. Tailor your jeans. It can be done, and it's worth every penny.

15. A cropped leather jacket will change your life.

14. Find five best friend pieces in your closet—the ones you want to hang out with. Your favorite sweater, your favorite shoe, your favorite dress. Treasure them!

13. Fast fashion is like fast food. It tastes great, and it can, once in a while, look great, but in the end, it's not really good for you.

12. This is super important: Find a fashion gay bestie. Yes, a fashion gay bestie.

11. Music is a must. Dance. People dance when you get dressed. Come on, shake it up!

10. Do not let your clothes dress you. If something's off, it's because the clothes are wearing you, not the other way around.

9. Juicy Couture is super underrated.

8. In the immortal words of Mommy Dearest: No more wire hangers.

7. Treat your closet like an investment, because it is!

6. If you consign something, make sure you empty your pockets. I've found money, engagement rings, paraphernalia and some photos. So empty 'em before you send 'em off.

5. Find a really good bag or shoe cobbler.

4. Say "Thursday" when taking a picture. Everybody together—Thursday. Cindy Crawford taught me that.

3. Fashion rules suck. There are no rules. Just make 'em up as you go along.

2. When in doubt, Prada. Enough said.

1. Reinvent yourself. It works for Madonna, it worked for me and it can work for you.

Chapter 7

In the early 2010s, *everyone* had a reality show.

It wasn't just socialites and party girls: I'd find myself looking around a dinner table or a club dance floor or a benefit gala and see them.

A hairstylist with a dramatic love life.

A workaholic house-flipper and interior designer.

Stylist-to-the-stars Rachel Zoe.

Stylist-to-the-stars Rachel Zoe's assistant Brad Goreski, who became a reality TV staple in his own right.

One of those nights, I asked myself a question I've been asking my entire life: Why not me?

I was funny, I had a glamorous business and I'd inherited more than a bit of Nick the Greek's charisma. Where was *my* reality show? It would be a hit! It was a persistent feeling, like an itch I couldn't scratch, telling me that my experiences in the fashion and business world could make for compelling television.

I was certain.

When I decided to dive into the world of reality

television, I had no idea what I was getting myself into. It was like jumping into a pool without checking if there was water in it first. Spoiler alert: there was water, but it was filled with piranhas and the occasional friendly goldfish. The reality TV world, as I soon discovered, was a bizarre ecosystem where drama was currency and authenticity was often left on the cutting room floor.

I pestered my agents relentlessly, probably to the point where they considered changing their phone numbers. But persistence paid off, and we landed four meetings with big networks.

To my surprise, they all said yes.

The networks were falling over themselves to get me on board, each promising bigger and better things. It was flattering, sure, but also a bit overwhelming. I felt like I had accidentally stumbled into a bidding war for my life. We ended up choosing Bravo, because who doesn't want to be associated with housewives flipping tables and wealthy people arguing on yachts?

Bravo seemed like the perfect fit—they had a knack for creating overnight sensations, and some of its stars were already people in my orbit.

Dukes of Melrose, as the show was called, officially entered production, I was ready for my close-up.

Or so I thought.

Lights, Camera, Action

Filming a reality show (while trying to have a real life) is not for the faint of heart. In 2012, while filming the show, I was working six days a week, which is not ideal if you're a mere mortal who occasionally needs sleep. The cameras were always rolling, catching every moment of triumph and disaster. There was no such thing as "off the record" anymore. Every conversation, every decision, every facial expression was potential fodder for the show.

The good news?

I lost 25 pounds.

The bad news?

I lost 25 pounds.

The constant pressure to be "on" and the long hours took their toll. I was running on adrenaline and determination, my body shedding weight as fast as I was shedding my privacy. Living in this reality TV twilight zone was like being in a constant state of paranoia. You start to question everything. Is that plant in the corner secretly a camera? Is my coffee mug recording our conversations?

The line between reality and "reality TV" became increasingly blurred. I found myself second-guessing every interaction, wondering how it would play out on screen. Would that offhand comment be taken out of context? Would that moment of frustration be blown out of proportion for dramatic effect?

And let's not forget the daily hair and makeup routine. Nothing says "I'm a serious businessman" like spending an hour in the makeup chair every morning. The glam squad became my constant companions, transforming me from a sleepy, stressed entrepreneur into a camera-ready version of myself. It was surreal to watch myself become a character in my own life, primped and polished for public consumption.

The experience was a crash course in the art of being constantly "on." Every day was a performance, a balancing act between being true to myself and giving the producers the drama they craved. It was exhausting, exhilarating and utterly bizarre.

Some days, I felt like I was swimming with the sharks. Other days, I was the shark, ruthlessly pursuing my goals in front of a national audience.

As the weeks went by, I began to understand the unwritten rules of reality TV. The camera loves conflict, so every disagreement becomes a potential storyline. Friendships are tested, loyalties are questioned and everything is fair game for the sake of good television. I found myself in situations I never imagined, having conversations I never thought I'd have on camera. I didn't know who to trust, and I'm sure other people working on the show and in my personal life felt the same about me, wondering what I'd be saying in my confessionals.

Looking back, I realize that diving into reality TV was like agreeing to live in a funhouse mirror version of my own life. Everything was slightly distorted, amplified for maximum effect. I emerged from the experience a different person—thinner, more media-savvy and with a newfound appreciation for the power of editing.

Hugs, Ego and Falling Through Floors

As the show started airing, weird things began to happen. First, people started recognizing me on the streets of New York. They'd come up to me saying, "Oh my God, I love your show. I love you, love you."

It was like being a rockstar, or at least like being the most popular kid in high school. I'd be walking down the street, minding my own business, maybe thinking about what to have for lunch, when suddenly I'd hear excited whispers and feel eyes on me. At first, I thought I must have forgotten to zip up my fly or had spinach stuck in my teeth. But no, it was just the bizarre reality of sudden fame.

People really wanted to hug me too, sometimes even in professional settings. They'd reach out to me, not to buy anything, but just to...hug. I felt like a human teddy bear. It was touching, literally and figuratively, but also a bit overwhelming. I mean, I went from being relatively unknown to suddenly being the most huggable person in Los Angeles and New York. Bravo fans are devoted—years later, I'd attend Bravocon, the network's annual convention, with my friend Garcelle, and the attention she and the other *Real Housewives of Beverly Hills* drew from the crowd was Beatlemania-esque.

My show had *just* premiered, and I was already getting recognized. Surely this was the start of a big TV career for me! The attention was intoxicating. I was trending on Twitter, which is equal parts exhilarating and terrifying. I'd wake up in the morning, check my phone, and see my name right up there with breaking news and celebrity gossip. It was surreal, like I had somehow hacked the matrix of pop culture and inserted myself into the public consciousness.

I also started believing my own hype. I'd catch

myself strutting down the street, thinking, "Yeah, that's right, I'm kind of a big deal." It was like I had developed an alter ego, "Reality TV Christos," who was slowly taking over.

But here's the thing about ego—it's like a balloon. The bigger it gets, the easier it is to pop. And eventually, did mine pop spectacularly. We had huge openings for the show in LA and New York. The LA event was like a who's who of Hollywood. My mom was there, beaming with pride and probably raiding the gift bags. I felt like I had finally arrived, like all those years of dreaming and working had finally paid off. I was rubbing elbows with celebrities as an equal, sipping champagne and basking in the glow of the spotlight. It was intoxicating, like being at the coolest party in town and realizing you're the guest of honor.

The New York event was even bigger. We had a massive space, and everyone who was anyone was there. I felt like I had finally made it to the New York glitterati. I was on top of the world, ready to give my speech and screen the first two episodes of the show. I had practiced my speech in the mirror, perfected my "I'm humbled but also fabulous" expression, and was ready to cement my status as the next big thing in reality TV.

On cue, I had what I can only describe as a "tetherball moment."

The screening equipment, moments before I was set to debut my show before friends, family and assorted New York celebrities, quit working. Here I was, at this massive event celebrating a show about my life, and the very technology that made it all possible was having a diva moment. I was fuming.

I stormed up to where my PR guy and creative team were, mic in hand, ready to unleash. I hurled the mic at my PR guy's head (sorry, Patrick! I'm glad you're still my PR guy all these years later!) and then, my face twisted in dramatic fury, I stepped and fell through a false landing on the stage.

One moment, I'm puffing up my shoulders like an angry Greek rooster, and the next, I'm doing an impromptu magic trick and disappearing through the floor. It was less "welcome to reality television" and more "welcome to America's Funniest Home Videos."

At that moment, as I was lying there, probably with a piece of the false floor stuck to my designer outfit, I had an epiphany. This was reality TV in its purest form—unscripted, unpredictable and humbling. It was a stark reminder that no matter how much we try to control our image or our narrative, life has a way of throwing curveballs (or in this case, collapsing floors) our way.

As I picked myself up, dusting off both my clothes and my ego, I couldn't help but laugh. Here I was, at the pinnacle of my reality TV career, and I had quite literally fallen from grace. It was a moment of pure, unscripted reality that no amount of editing could smooth over. And in a weird way, it was liberating to be reminded that while I may have been a reality TV star, I was still me. The show, as I knew it would be, was canceled quicker than a *Housewives* marriage, but it was quite a ride while it lasted.

Watching What Happens

One of the perks of being on a Bravo show is getting invited to make an appearance on *Watch What Happens Live*, the late-night Bravo talk show hosted by the impresario of reality TV, Andy Cohen. It's like being invited to the cool kids' table in the cafeteria, except the cool kids are Housewives and the celebrities who love them. This late-night talk show is the epicenter of Bravo's reality TV universe, where stars collide, drama unfolds and the drinks flow freely.

I found myself doing *shot-skis* with Christian Siriano, the Project Runway winner and superstar designer who I've known forever. For those uninitiated in the ways of Andy Cohen's clubhouse, a *shot-ski* is exactly what it sounds like—a ski with shot glasses attached to it. It's like the winter sports version of a drinking game. Imagine a long wooden ski with several shot glasses glued to it at regular intervals. The idea is that multiple people lift the ski together and take their shots simultaneously. It's part drinking game, part trust exercise and entirely ridiculous in the best possible way.

Looking back at the video, I have to say, I was pretty funny. My tanner was on point, my hair was perfectly dyed and my suit was red. It's a strange experience watching yourself on TV, especially when you're trying to be witty and charming while also worrying about whether your fake tan is streaking under the hot studio lights.

The pressure of live television is intense. Every word, every gesture is broadcast to millions of homes across the country. One wrong move, one ill-timed joke, and you could become the next viral meme or Twitter scandal. It's a high-wire act that requires quick wit, charm and the ability to hold your liquor while being peppered with questions about the latest reality TV drama.

The experience was a whirlwind of laughter, nerves and alcohol. Andy Cohen, ever the gracious host, has a knack for making his guests feel at ease while also gently prodding them for juicy tidbits. It's like being interrogated by your most charming friend, who just happens to have an audience of millions.

It was surreal to be on the other side of the TV screen. I kept expecting someone to tap me on the shoulder and say, "Sorry, there's been a mistake. We meant to invite the other Christos. You know, the one who's actually famous." This impostor syndrome is a common feeling for many people thrust into the spotlight, but it's particularly acute when you're sitting in Andy Cohen's colorful clubhouse, surrounded by people you've watched on TV for years.

A "Eureka" Moment

While I was busy trying not to look directly into the reality TV cameras, I was also working on my ultimate dream: getting a fashion line on the Home Shopping Network.

You might be wondering, "Why HSN?"

As a 10-year-old gay kid, I was obsessed with watching skincare guru Adrien Arpel change lives and make money on TV. While other kids were dreaming of becoming astronauts or firefighters, I was dreaming of selling moisturizer to middle-aged women at 2 am. Dream big, kids! Adrien was my idol. I'd watch her, mesmerized, as she effortlessly convinced viewers that they absolutely needed that revolutionary new face cream or that life-changing cleanser. It was like watching a master class in persuasion and showmanship, all wrapped up in a perfectly coiffed package.

HSN was the promised land, a place where dreams were sold in convenient installment plans, and where a charismatic personality could become a household name faster than you can say "But wait, there's more!" The first credit card I got when I was 18 years old, in college, had a $200 limit on it. And you know what my first purchase was? You would think I'd do something fun, like drinks at a club. I bought pillows on the Home Shopping Network. That's how obsessed I was with it, and when that box of throw pillows arrived, I was like a little kid on Christmas morning.

So, while I was filming the reality show, I was simultaneously working on my HSN pitch. I was in a hurry to nail it, because the show was kind of a flop and I knew even before the first season was over that I probably wouldn't be getting renewed.

The process of developing my HSN pitch was a journey in itself. I spent countless hours refining my product line, making sure each piece had a story, a unique selling point that would make it irresistible to the HSN audience. I practiced my pitch in front of mirrors, I studied the HSN greats, analyzing their techniques, their catchphrases, the way they could make even the most mundane product sound like a must-have item.

My agent, Pilar, was my shining light through this whole process. Her father managed Madonna and Michael Jackson, so clearly, dealing with my HSN dreams was a piece of cake compared to handling the King and Queen of Pop. Pilar was a force of nature, a whirlwind of connections and negotiations. She believed in my vision when others might have dismissed it as just another reality star trying to cash in on their 15 minutes of fame.

Pilar's experience in the entertainment industry was invaluable. She knew how to navigate the complex world of television contracts, how to pitch to the right people, and most importantly, how to keep me grounded when the stress of juggling reality TV and HSN preparations threatened to overwhelm me. She was part agent, part therapist and part drill sergeant, pushing me to refine my pitch, expand my product line and never lose sight of the end goal.

With Pilar's guidance, we put together a pitch package that was impossible to ignore. We had mood boards, product samples and a presentation that could make even the most jaded TV executive sit up and take notice. It was a perfect blend of my design aesthetic, my personality and the HSN formula for success.

In 2012, while I was planning my HSN pitch, my Bravo show was canceled, and I knew there was a sense of urgency at hand—the network might be less interested in me if they knew I no longer had a platform of my own. As we prepared for the big pitch meeting, I felt like I was standing on the precipice of something huge. This was more than just a business opportunity; it was the culmination of a childhood dream, a chance to step into the shoes of my idol Adrien Arpel and carve out my own niche in the world of home shopping.

I put together a portfolio of my ideas with a designer friend of mine. It was like creating a fashion-forward version of a high school project, except instead of a grade, I was hoping for a national platform to sell my designs. We spent countless hours poring over sketches, fabric swatches and mood boards. It was a delicate balance, trying to create something that was uniquely "me" while also appealing to the HSN audience. I wanted to bring high fashion to the masses, but in a way that was accessible and relatable.

The fashion world is small, and the home shopping world even smaller. It felt like every conversation, every networking event, every chance encounter could be the one that led to my big break.

The pitch meeting was my chance to shine, to show them what I was all about. I channeled all my years of watching Adrien Arpel and prepared to dazzle them. I was tap dancing like my life depended on it. It was like being back in my Clorox job interview, but with more sequins and less bleach. I presented my designs, my vision, my brand with all the enthusiasm and charm I could muster. I was selling not just clothes, but a story—my story. Every piece had a tale behind it, every collection a theme that tied into my experiences and my aesthetic.

To my surprise, they recognized the work of the designer I had collaborated with. It was like accidentally name-dropping a celebrity and finding out the person you're talking to is their best friend. This unexpected connection added an extra layer of credibility to my pitch.

They loved the concept, inspired by the high-end pieces I'd spent years discovering in celebrity closets. We called it "Eureka by Christos Garkinos" because nothing says "I've found it!" like a Greek exclamation. The idea was to bring the thrill of discovery, the joy of finding that perfect piece, to the HSN audience. Each item would have a story, a reason why it was special and why the viewer needed it in their life.

The HSN team could see the potential for storytelling, for creating a connection with the audience. In the world of home shopping, it's not just about the product—it's about the narrative you weave around it.

And I had stories in spades.

Walking out of that initial meeting, I felt like I was floating. The reality of it hadn't quite sunk in yet. Here I was, on the verge of achieving a dream I'd had since childhood. The excitement was palpable. My mind was already racing with ideas for new collections, for segments, for how I would present myself on air. I imagined myself standing there, under the bright lights, talking to millions of viewers about my designs, my inspirations, my journey.

It was terrifying and thrilling in equal measure.

As we left the building, Pilar and I were already strategizing. We needed to start planning the collections, thinking about production, considering how we'd balance this new venture with my existing commitments. It was going to be a juggling act, but one I was more than ready to take on.

The reality TV world had given me a taste of fame, but this—this was something different. This was a chance to build something lasting, to create a brand that could live beyond the fleeting attention span of reality television. It was an opportunity to connect with people in their homes, to be a part of their lives in a tangible way.

The HSN Debut: Dreams Do Come True (Sometimes, in Sequins)

Walking onto the HSN set for the first time was a surreal experience. It was a perfect blend of retro chic and modern elegance, reflecting the aesthetic—with my name in lights, of course—I had always dreamed of for my brand. Every detail, from the lighting to the display cases, was meticulously crafted to showcase the designs in the best possible way.

My sister was one of the models, and seeing her there, wearing my designs, brought a lump to my throat. It was a tangible reminder of how far we'd come from Michigan. She wasn't the only Greek there, of course.

Being Greek, as you probably know by now, is incredibly important to me. I'm so proud of my ancestors near and far, and of the indomitable Greek spirit that has, for my entire life, motivated me to do and seek more. I'm also aware of how much Greeks love to support other Greeks, so in advance of my official debut on HSN, I visited Greek churches all around the country, drumming up enthusiasm and, in many cases, ensuring certain pieces would sell out before they even hit the screen.

Each item in the collection was more than just a piece of clothing; it was a narrative, a slice of my life and experiences transformed into wearable art. From the inspirations behind each design to the unique details that made them special, I had a story ready for every single piece.

I named clothes after some of my celebrity friends. It was like playing a grown-up version of house, but instead of naming dolls, I was naming clothes that real people could buy and wear. “Oh, you like this jacket? It’s called the ‘Jody Watley.’ And this dress? That’s the ‘Garcelle Beauvais.’” It was my way of paying homage to the people who had supported me throughout my journey, and it added an extra layer of glamor and intrigue to the collection.

The support was overwhelming. Some of my celebrity friends called in, probably a little bemused at this alternate universe where I was a TV shopping mogul. But there I was, selling out my entire line on the first day. The phones were ringing off the hook, the items were flying off the shelves, and I was in the middle of it all, trying to keep my cool while internally screaming.

The energy on set was electric. The crew, the models, even the camera operators seemed to be caught up in the excitement. It was as if we were all riding this wave of success together, each sale, each call, each sold-out item adding to the collective euphoria.

The first item went live—a distressed piece—and it

sold out instantly. The second item, a blouse, sold out just as quickly.

Then came...the pants.

Let me tell you, if there's anything harder to sell on live TV, it's basic black pants. And I had 3,000 of these pants to sell.

I was thinking, "How on earth am I going to sell these?"

The only unique thing about them was this seam down the side. It was designed to create a slimming effect, kind of like the illusion of the Sleeping Beauty castle at Disneyland—it looks huge from a distance but gets smaller as you approach. That seam somehow made the pants look slimmer.

But still, they were black pants.

How do I make people want these? And then, something just clicked. Maybe it was instinct. I dropped to my knees next to my co-host, Colleen Lopez—the Oprah of HSN—and I traced my finger from the top of her pelvic bone (without actually touching her, of course) down the seam of the pants, all the way toward her ankle in the most dramatic—and yeah, erotic—way I could muster.

Before I even reached her ankle, she exclaimed, "And we sold out!"

We had sold out all 3,000 pairs. I couldn't believe it.

My face must have been priceless—complete shock. Colleen was stunned, too. The models were high-fiving me. I was suddenly the hottest thing on HSN, and the whole experience felt absolutely electric. (And PS: I ended up meeting Adrien Arpel—can you even imagine what a moment that was?)

But even in the midst of this triumph, there was a small voice in the back of my mind, a whisper of caution. Success, I was learning, could be as unpredictable as it was exhilarating. For now, though, I pushed that voice aside.

This was my moment, and I was determined to savor every second of it.

On Top...For Now

When I first got training for HSN, I had been watching the network religiously since I was 10, so I thought I knew what to expect. There were two other big-name designers there for training with me, and I wasn't even a designer—I was just a curator. But somehow, I stole the show. When I got up there, it just came naturally. I could hear clipboards dropping in the background, and people whispering, *Who is this person?*

My HSN debut was a smashing success. I had a total sellout on my first day. It was like being a rock star, but instead of groupies, I had enthusiastic shoppers calling in to buy my designs. It got to the point where they even asked me to train the other designers on how to sell. Can you imagine? Me, training these established names! It was surreal, but it felt like I was made for this.

I was riding high, thinking, "This is it! I'm going to be the next big thing in home shopping!"

The adrenaline rush was intoxicating. Every ring of

the phone, every sold-out item, felt like a standing ovation.

They brought me back for a second round, and boom —another sellout. I was on fire. In my mind, I was already planning my HSN empire (with fewer plastic surgery jokes and more actual fashion). I could see it all so clearly: a Fashion Week special, a red-carpet collection, "Christos" spelled out in even bigger and brighter lights.

The possibilities seemed endless. Don't they always?

But here's the thing about life—it has a way of keeping you humble. Just when you think you're about to take off and soar, it clips your wings and reminds you that you're still very much human.

I'm a Gemini, and I've always innately understood the concept of a double life. There was the Christos who showed up to every HSN taping, full of life and excitement and ready to sell black pants or sequined jackets or some combination of the two.

Then there was...the other Christos. It's probably time I introduce you to him, so get ready.

I certainly wasn't.

Chapter 8

For years, I'd felt like an outsider looking in, like that guy who always seemed to be stuck at the kids' table. I had achieved almost everything I ever set out to do, and then some. I hadn't just met my idols—I'd become friends with them. It's so cliche I almost hate to admit it, but in my case it was true: I spent so much of my life with my nose pressed up against the glass of what I thought I wanted.

Once I got to the other side, it was quite a shock to realize I didn't actually feel like a different person.

There was this gnawing feeling deep down that kept whispering, "This is too good to be true. Any minute now, you're going to trip over your own ego and face-plant into reality."

Would anyone have guessed my secret? Looked at me and known that deep down, I was still that gay, too-smart-for-his-own-good Greek kid from Michigan, looking for a way to fit in with the all-American blondes of Grosse Pointe?

Probably not. I had a husband of 10 years, I was on TV, and when I wasn't hosting live shows featuring my own line on HSN, I was styling celebrity friends and clients, and being photographed in designer suits at LA events. The lights of Hollywood seemed like they sparkled around me.

Lights can be blinding, though, and in my case, even I had a hard time seeing what was really happening.

Where Everyone Knows Your Name

Let's back up a little bit.

I went to a lot of parties and events during my time at Virgin Megastore, and—as Janet Jackson can attest to —I drank my fair share of champagne. Still, I wouldn't have classified myself as a *partier*, in no small part because I've always been a 24/7, 365 kind of guy when it comes to work.

In 2013, when my HSN line debuted and immediately sold out, I thought I was on top of the world—or at least, that's how it felt. I had just wrapped up a successful run on a reality show and was thriving as part of HSN. Life seemed perfect, and my ego was running the show. Then, of course, reality came knocking. That's when I stumbled into Giorgio's, a nightclub that would change everything.

Giorgio's wasn't just any club; it was an escape. Named after the legendary Giorgio Moroder, it became my sanctuary during a time when I desperately needed a release. I was in my late 40s, almost 50, and ready to dive into a new lifestyle of late nights and endless music.

My friend Carlota had told me about the place. "You have to come," they insisted.

The club itself was tucked away in the back of the Standard Hotel on Sunset Boulevard. You had to walk through the kitchen to get there—a tiny, intimate space that only held about 150 people. No cameras were allowed, so people—even big-deal celebrities—felt at ease, ready and game for anything. It was just pure, unfiltered freedom.

I still remember the night I first walked in. Bobby Caldwell's "What You Won't Do for Love" was playing—one of my favorite songs. The smooth, blue-eyed soul wrapped around me like a warm hug. In that moment, I knew: This was where I belonged. It reminded me of the disco and R&B scenes I dreamed about as a kid, only now including a seat at a VIP table and a never-ending supply of drinks.

From that night on, Giorgio's became my ritual. Every Saturday, I'd show up at 10:30 pm and dance until 4 am. I became a regular—no, an addict.

Giorgio's was where I reconnected with myself and, ironically, where I met husband number two. At the time, I was going with my friend Jody Watley, a Grammy winning performer I'd loved since my teen years. We had our own little velvet area in the back, our personal haven. Celebrities would come by, joining us in our makeshift VIP corner, and the nights that unfolded there were unforgettable.

There's something magical about dancing in a circle with people you admire. One night, it was me, Jody, Lisa Stansfield ("All Around the World") and Siobhan Fahey from Bananarama. I couldn't believe it—Lisa Stansfield was huge to me! I had loved her music since the '90s, and there she was, right in front of me, dancing like there was no tomorrow. She was wild in the best way, the kind of person who'd unapologetically smoke in an elevator. That night, surrounded by legends, I thought, *This is it—I could die happy right now.*

Mick Jagger walked in once, and the whole club tilted sideways. Celebrities melting down, celebrities cutting loose—it was a constant spectacle. I even found myself teaching the *Saturday Night Live* superstar Amy Poehler how to "whack," a dance style that predated voguing. There I was, whacking around Amy Poehler on the dance floor, her expression a mix of confusion and delight. I'll never forget it. It was one of those surreal, only-at-Giorgio's moments.

But the club wasn't just a haven for celebrity encounters; it was where I rediscovered myself. Growing up gay and straddling two cultures—Greek and American—I'd always felt like an outsider. Giorgio's was the first place where I felt like I truly belonged. Fashion, music, connection—it all fused together here in a way that made sense to me. For someone who had always felt alone in a crowd, Giorgio's became my crowd. It gave me a sense of belonging when I needed it most, a place where my love for fashion, music and connection could thrive. And even though my time there was marked by both joy and heartache, it remains part of one of the most defining chapters of my life.

One night, I was dancing with my friend. This guy walked in and I looked at him and I said to myself and to her, "Oh my God, I'm in trouble." Something about him stopped me in my tracks.

I just knew it.

He knew it, too, and he actually asked me once: "Are you sure you want this?"

I knew the right answer was "no," but I overruled myself, and there we were.

Loss and Lost

Around this time, my husband Brett—the first one (and still, thankfully, one of my best friends)—and I were living in Hancock Park, one of LA's loveliest and most historic neighborhoods. We had converted a garage lovingly dubbed WIT, which stood for "Women in Transition." It was where friends would come and stay when they were dealing with bad breakups or job losses or health issues. This was my way of giving back, a little sanctuary for friends going through rough patches.

Cathy, my best friend and practically my sister, had moved in with us to battle a rare form of cancer. We'd known each other for decades; she was my rock, and I was determined to be hers. It was supposed to be a happy, if challenging, chapter. I would be there for Cathy as she worked her way up to full strength, and then, together, we'd reemerge from our cocoon back into the world, ready to take on whatever was next for us.

One April day, Cathy called, her voice weak but hopeful. I took her to the hospital, and within five days, I was holding her hand as she took her last breath.

And just like that, I felt my world crumble. I walked

out of Cedars-Sinai Hospital and I left my whole world behind.

I went downstairs into the lobby with my husband and the two friends who were there with us when Cathy died, and I looked at everybody and just said, "I have to get out of here."

And I literally pretty much walked out of my marriage that day and into a new life.

In retrospect, I see now that this was how I'd always coped with loss—by running away.

Loss has been a theme that's loomed over my entire life, and the way I've learned to navigate it has continuously shaped who I am. I can clearly remember the first time it hit me in a way that felt truly irreparable. It was 1992, and I was living in Los Angeles. I was 28, just making my way in life, and then my father passed away. I was still grieving the loss of one of my best friends, who had died exactly one year earlier, almost to the day.

The pain was unbearable, suffocating even, and the sense of abandonment stuck with me.

You know how they say you have two options when faced with tragedy—fight or flee? Well, I fled. I couldn't deal with the grief, so I did what felt right at the time: I left. Sure, it was a "geographic," a term in sober circles that addresses the idea of physically moving to escape your problems. It's funny how you can do all that running, but the real issues inside you remain, no matter where you land. But I didn't know that then.

It wasn't until much later that this pattern became more apparent. Every time I encountered loss, I would start over, but those fresh starts didn't mean I had processed the grief. Take London, for example. It was another geographic, another fresh start. I threw myself into work. I was going to Paris every other weekend and manifesting opportunities—like the time I kept telling myself, "I want to work for Virgin," and then ended up in my dream job. That manifestation and that job did change my life, but they didn't fix what was broken, because, for so long, I didn't even really understand that something *was* broken.

I threw myself headfirst into two new relationships: one was with this guy from Giorgio's and the other was with drugs.

At age 50, I had never tried cocaine before, even though I'd seen people do plenty of it. I knew it was something that would be a problem for me, so I stayed away—until I didn't. Let me be clear: until this point, I was never a heavy drinker or drug user. But there's something about hitting rock bottom that makes you think, "Hey, why not dive headfirst into the abyss?" It didn't help that my new boyfriend was, in many ways, similar to my father: handsome, incredibly charismatic and just a little bit damaged.

I can fix him, I thought to myself, and in trying to do so, I found myself stuck on a merry-go-round of trying to make it work with someone unworkable.

Within months, I went from trying cocaine to liking cocaine to loving cocaine, and before I knew it, I was a full-blown addict. From 2014 to mid-2016, my life was a blur of reckless decisions and misguided escapades. It was like I was living in a never-ending party where the music was great, but the hangover was always around the corner.

Last Call

My real friends didn't know what to make of the new me. They'd look at me and say, "What the fuck is going on with you?" And honestly, I didn't know. I'd left my old life behind because I couldn't handle the pain I was causing, but the decisions I made after that only spiraled further out of control.

I was in such a bad headspace, and it affected everything. I got married to my Giorgio's boyfriend quickly, almost impulsively, like I was trying to prove something to the world—or maybe to myself. But instead of fixing anything, it sent me deeper into a dark place. For almost two-and-a-half years, I was trapped in that cycle. Coke became a regular thing, and so did Adderall. I spent hundreds of thousands of dollars on drugs, on parties—it was an escape, but it wasn't sustainable. I moved into an expensive rental house at the top of Mulholland Drive, the sweeping views of LA serving as the backdrop for cocaine binges and parties that never seemed to end.

Looking back, I think part of it was rebellion. I was such a good kid growing up. I was the teacher's pet, always working hard, doing the right thing. But there was this part of me—a gremlin, I guess—that had been waiting to come out. And when it did, it wreaked havoc on everything. My family noticed, my friends noticed, my work suffered. People didn't understand what was going on with me. They didn't know how to connect with me anymore.

In the middle of all that, I isolated myself. My social circle became his friends—people tied to that lifestyle. I didn't have any real support. The people who truly cared about me were stepping away, and I can't blame them. I was making stupid decisions, one after the other. I even went to my therapist, sat down and said, "My life's out of control. I don't know how to fix it." And honestly, neither did they.

It all started to fall apart when the money began to run out. One by one, everything I had built started to crumble.

My deal with HSN came to an end—that devastated me, because it had been a lifelong dream. It wasn't even that I was doing a bad job so much as that I was trying almost too hard to prove that I was supposed to be there. The audience can sense when you're trying too hard, and my most recent collection didn't do so well. Since you're only as hot as your last collection, they politely let me know that my contract wasn't being renewed.

A TV project I had been filming fell through and my manager Pilar parted ways with me. I was up for a huge gig at Access Hollywood but that didn't happen either. Suddenly, nothing was going my way.

My whole life had been about manifesting success, about things working out, but this was the opposite. And I wasn't doing anything to stop it—I was negligent, spiraling, unhappy. I kept shutting people out, recreating the trauma from my past in some weird, self-destructive way. Some of my closest friends obviously knew something was very wrong: I remember, after one night out, my longtime friend Monet Mazur, a talented actress, dropped me off at my house, and she paused as we were saying goodbye.

"Are you...okay?" she asked.

I sensed that she didn't want to let me go inside because she felt just how not okay I was.

I brushed her off and retreated into my bubble. The energy around me at this point was cold—like I was frozen in a block of ice, unable to receive the love and kindness of even the people closest to me.

Typical addict behavior, right?

You retreat into a corner, isolate yourself and refuse to let anyone in. That's exactly what I was doing. For several years, well into 2016, things got progressively worse. The relationship I was in lasted longer than it should have, dragging me down with it.

But the lowest point came later. It's something I talk about now in my AA meetings, this idea that it has to get worse before it gets better.

For me, it got much, much worse.

I was living a complete lie. Everything about my life was a facade, held together by addiction and denial. The breaking point came during a massive fight with my husband at the time. It was one of those moments where everything shatters, and you're left looking at the pieces, wondering how it all went so wrong. But even then, I wasn't ready to face it.

He wanted to leave, I wanted him to leave, I didn't want him to leave. I was terrified of being abandoned once again—of having more irrefutable proof that I was the problem. One dramatic night, I threw myself onto the driveway of our opulent Mulholland estate, refusing to let him leave. He drove up to where I lay and revved the engine.

I was so far gone that I thought, "Please, just end it. I can't bear this anymore."

I don't know whether or not I actually wanted him to run me over—and I'm certainly glad that he didn't—but I wanted and needed, so badly, for something to change. For something to happen, for better or for worse.

It was around Greek Easter, just a couple of days before the holiday. That week, I had agreed to host a party at my house for 100 people to celebrate my friend Katie's book release. The timing couldn't have been worse. I was a complete mess, barely holding myself together. Despite my internal chaos, I went through with it. Somehow, I managed to host the party, but no one understood the depth of what I was experiencing.

Then the season of Greek Easter arrived, bringing another fight into my already fragile existence. I had planned to host 50 people the next day, with the backyard perfectly decorated in hues of blue and white, in the traditional Greek style, so I could show off my fabulous heritage to my fabulous friends in the hope that everything would seem so fabulous that no one would notice what was really happening.

But I couldn't do it. I canceled the gathering. That decision marked the beginning of a profound shift in my life. That was the day—April 30th, 2016—that I would hit rock bottom and, unknowingly, the night I would start my journey to sobriety.

I had my dog, Sophie, with me that weekend. She was a shared companion between my ex-husband Brett and me, and I was looking after her for a few days. It was the night before Greek Easter, and the house was dark and eerily silent. Instead of celebrating with my friends, I was alone, doing blow, spiraling further into despair. Three in the morning came and with it, the dawn of Easter in Michigan.

I decided to call my mom to wish her a happy Easter. I was completely high, but I tried to act normal. She could sense something was off, but she didn't know what; I had made sure to keep my problems a secret from her.

"What's wrong?" she asked, her voice filled with concern.

"It's nothing," I replied, brushing off her worries. "Everything's fine."

But everything wasn't fine.

I hung up the phone and stared at my surroundings. My stash was running low, so I started digging through the garbage, desperate for more. That's when it hit me—a moment of clarity, or perhaps disgust. I was almost 52 years old, digging through the trash looking for drugs. Was this my life?

I froze.

"What are you doing? What the fuck are you *doing?*"

The weight of that question crushed me.

I sat down in front of my computer, completely broken. I don't remember exactly what I typed in, but I typed, hoping the Internet would send me some kind of sign.

I ended up stopping a video of a Greek Orthodox church service. The hymns, the soundtrack of so much of my childhood, filled the room, and something stirred within me. It wasn't a grand revelation, but a quiet, insistent thought: I can't do this anymore.

For a fleeting moment, I wasn't sure if I was going to take my own life or if something miraculous was about to happen. I didn't know what the next step would be, but I knew I couldn't keep going like this.

I finally passed out from sheer exhaustion, and when I woke up the next morning, it was May 1st, and for the first time in years, I was sober. I felt awful—physically, emotionally, spiritually—but I was clear-headed enough to make a decision. I called Brett and told him, "You need to come get the dog. I don't know what's going to happen to me."

He arrived with my best friend, Kelly, who took one look at me and said, "We love you, and we know you need help." They saved my life that day. I began intensive therapy, and May 1, 2016 became my sobriety date. I declared it to myself and some of the people closest to me. The days that followed were grueling.

I began attending meetings, stepping into rooms filled with strangers and admitting, "I'm an alcoholic." Those words felt like they were slicing through me. I cried—a lot. I leaned into therapy, sometimes going twice a day, and poured my pain into the process. The separation from my husband only added to the weight I was carrying, but I kept moving forward. I was grappling with the existential question of why this was happening to me.

How this could have happened to me. Everything had gone my way for 50 years—and now it hadn't.

I didn't know then that I was about to live through the most challenging moment of my life.

The Hardest Goodbye

I didn't tell many people in my life I had gotten sober: not even my mom.

I was still married at the time, trying to figure out my relationship while navigating sobriety. My partner wasn't sober, and that made everything harder. I wanted to save him, and I wanted to save myself, and I wanted to see if there was anything worth salvaging in our marriage—but with my own sobriety so fragile, I didn't know how I was going to move forward.

About six weeks into my sobriety, I had to go back to Michigan because my mom was having elective heart surgery. She was strong and healthy, but there was a minor issue with her heart—a little blockage that required a minor procedure to place two stents. It didn't seem like a big deal. Just a quick fix.

When I got there, I was struggling. Six weeks sober and barely holding it together, I found myself fighting with my then-husband more than ever. I was barely even focused on the surgery. It felt like I was juggling a thousand things—my sobriety, my failing marriage and now, my mom's health. In body, I was there, but in spirit?

Who even knows.

The day of the surgery arrived, and I remember sitting with my sister in the waiting area, staring at the monitors. In surgery, they use a color system—red means the patient is still in surgery, green means they're done and recovering. When her surgery turned green, I thought, "Okay, great, she's coming out."

But then, suddenly, it flipped back to red.

"What's going on?" we asked.

Hours passed, and the tension was unbearable. Then the doctors came out and explained: she'd bled out during surgery. They managed to stabilize her, but barely. She held on for two days, and then she was gone. My sister and I were in the room with her, and as I played a song by The Commodores called "Zoom" that reminded me of my mom and how much I loved her, she passed.

Just like that, my mom, Aspasia Garkinos, the strongest person I knew, was gone.

I was devastated. My mom was my world—I'm a mama's boy through and through. Everything I did was to make her proud—now what? Sitting there in that hospital, it didn't feel real. I remember thinking, "What the fuck just happened?"

I couldn't even begin to wrap my mind around the reality of the situation: I was never going to hear her voice again. I was never going to bring her to a party as my date, beaming as she worked the room like a pro. No more middle-of-the-night pep talks, no more "just thinking of you" calls, no more *home*—because that's what she was to me. My home.

Gone.

And there I was—six weeks sober, grieving, lost and wondering what the hell I was supposed to do now. I didn't know how to process any of it, so I just...kept going. One day at a time, they say.

Then, as if losing my mom wasn't enough, life decided to pile it on. Within two months, I lost two of my aunts—women who were like second mothers to me. They were my anchors in the wake of my mom's passing, and now they were gone, too.

And then, I kid you not: my dog died.

Despite loss being my kryptonite, I trudged onward barreling through the losses. Not fleeing.

I was also, thanks to the several years I'd spent partying, on the brink of bankruptcy. My business collapsed, and everything I'd worked for seemed to slip through my fingers. My finances were in shambles. I emptied my 401(K) just to stay afloat, but even that wasn't enough.

Eventually, I couldn't take my marriage anymore. It was toxic, suffocating. We divorced, which felt like the right thing to do, but was still devastating. There I was, newly sober and facing the reality of starting over—alone.

Yay, sobriety, I thought bitterly.

It felt like a cruel joke.

I ended up living in this huge, empty house that I couldn't afford. The lease wasn't up yet, so I was stuck. My money was dwindling, and I couldn't keep up with the lifestyle I'd been desperately trying to maintain.

By 2017, I was still in that house, trying to figure it all out. My life felt like a series of never-ending punches, each one landing harder than the last. I spent so much time driving around aimlessly, just trying to escape the crushing loneliness.

There were moments I wanted to give up, to throw in the towel and let the chaos win. But somehow, I didn't. Maybe it was sheer stubbornness, or maybe it was the faint hope that things would eventually get better.

And slowly, they did.

Sobriety didn't magically fix everything—it wasn't some instant ticket to happiness. But it gave me the clarity to face the wreckage of my life head-on. It forced me to sit with my pain, my grief, my failures, and find a way through them.

I started to rebuild, piece by piece.

There were no shortcuts, no easy answers. But I realized that surviving those dark moments proved something to myself: I was stronger than I'd ever given myself credit for. And while the losses still hurt—my mom, my aunts, my dog, my marriage, my money—I learned that grief doesn't have to consume you.

Sobriety, for all its challenges, became my anchor. It didn't take away the pain, but it gave me the tools to navigate it. And for that, I'm grateful.

I'm proud to say that, since May 1, 2016, I've remained sober, and plan on doing so for the rest of my life.

Chapter 9

Somehow, some way, I managed to stay sober through the passing of my mom, and later, my aunts and my dog.

I managed to stay sober through a divorce.

I also managed to stay sober through moving out of that giant house on top of Mulholland and into a small apartment in the heart of Hollywood, on a less-than-glamorous street filled with apartments crammed with 26-year-olds just moving to LA and hoping for a break.

I had my sobriety, but I didn't have much else.

I was in a lot of debt—like, half a million dollars' worth of debt. I was driving around the city, alone, in a leased Range Rover I couldn't really afford but also couldn't even sell, going to meetings and crying and trying to figure out where the last few years had gone and what exactly I was going to do now.

Seriously, I thought almost every day back then: how is this my life? Is this my life? How did I come this far only to lose it all? Was I, after 30 years of a high-flying career in music and fashion and TV, going to have to say goodbye to LA (and New York and Paris and London) and move back to *Michigan?*

The ultimate Hollywood cliché.

I did the only thing any smart, sane, rational person would have done in that moment: I signed up for Match.com.

The Match

It's hard to say now what I was looking for when I decided, in 2017, to sign up for a dating website—Match.com. I know I was lonely, having parted ways with my second husband (an aside: am I the most legally-divorced gay man in America?) and many of our mutual friends. My own closest friends had stuck by my side, but they had their own lives going on, and I was spending most of my time alone.

Scrolling one day, I was stopped in my tracks by a picture of a handsome African-American man. He looked a lot younger than me, but there was something about him—I needed to know more.

Rolland came into my life at a time when everything felt unsteady. Younger than me, he was somehow grounded in ways I couldn't quite grasp. He carried himself with a calm sense of purpose. He went to church every Sunday, an unwavering ritual in his life, and he loved to share these little "isms" with me daily—small nuggets of wisdom and encouragement that, at the time, felt like lifelines.

Rolland was so loving, so giving and so supportive. We both loved fashion and reality TV and had lots in common despite the age difference. I was broke as hell and newly sober. I felt like I had nothing to give him, but what mattered was his presence—steady, reliable and kind.

One day, Rolland said something that stayed with me. He told me, "I don't even know if we're going to work out, but I know you need a friend right now." And when we met, I thought, *Whatever this is going to be, I just know this person has been placed in my life because he needs a friend.* And he was right—I did need a friend.

In many ways, Rolland became that friend when I least expected it—and, since I was least expecting it, he also became the love of my life.

It wasn't just Rolland, though. My other friends rallied around me during this difficult chapter of my life. They showed up for me in ways I will never forget, providing the stability I desperately needed. These friends, old and new, formed a kind of protective circle around me, reminding me that I wasn't as alone as I felt.

In the middle of all this, I was doing whatever I could to keep moving forward. I was taking pet-sitting jobs wherever I could find them. A hundred dollars here, a hundred dollars there—every little bit helped. I was selling my own clothes at flea markets. I was just trying to stay afloat while also mourning the loss of my mom, a grief so heavy it felt impossible to carry some days. There's something about losing your mom that shifts everything. Mothers have this way of knowing you, sometimes better than you know yourself. I didn't fully realize that until after she was gone.

One memory in particular sticks with me. Before my

mom went into what was supposed to be that easy, routine surgery that took her life, she turned to my sister. I wasn't in the room at the time—I was still in the waiting area. But she looked my sister in the eye and said, "No matter what happens, if I don't come out of this, make sure he gets out of that relationship and gets help."

She was talking about my second husband—while I hadn't told her much about the reality of my situation at that time, and I certainly hadn't told her about the drugs, she was certain I wasn't where I supposed to be, and she was worried about me.

She didn't know the full extent of what I was going through, but somehow, she knew enough. Those were her last words before the surgery. My sister didn't tell me this until a year after my mom passed away. By then, I was already in the process of getting divorced, navigating the painful but necessary journey toward reclaiming my life.

Looking back, I'm so grateful my sister waited to share that with me. If she had told me then, when the grief was still so raw and my world was crumbling, I would have relapsed. I'm certain of it. Instead, when I finally heard my mom's last wish, it felt like confirmation. It was as if she had been watching over me, guiding me even in her absence. That knowledge—that her final thoughts were of me and my well-being—gave me a strange kind of strength. It was bittersweet, knowing how much she worried about me, but it also reminded me of how deeply she loved me.

So, I kept going. I leaned on my friends. I built

something new with Rolland. I grieved my mom. I did what I had to do to keep moving forward, step by painful step.

And through it all, I held on to her words—not just the ones she spoke but the unspoken ones that echoed in my heart: You're stronger than you think.

Keep going. There was bound to be a comeback.

The Spark

By 2018, I was in a relationship with Rolland, every day feeling incredibly grateful that this warm, fashionable, handsome, one-of-a-kind man had come into my life.

I was also still flat broke, which was terrifying. I'd been working and making money since I was a kid, at times supporting not just myself but my family, and to be in a position where I genuinely didn't know how I was going to make it to the next month made it hard to get through the day, let alone visualize what my future might look like.

I do believe, though, that the universe sends us lifelines when we need them the most, because it sent one to me in the form of a woman I met in—and this is so on-the-nose it almost feels made up—Detroit, Michigan. The city of my birth, and in some ways, the city of my re-birth.

I was down to my last dollars, checking my bank account's balance every day, trying to figure out how I was going to pay rent and make a dent in the now close-to $400,000 I owed.

A friend-of-a-friend reached out and said, "Hey, we

have a gig for you." She explained what they needed: "Would you go host a dinner for us in Detroit? You're from Detroit, right? It'll be at a hotel, and we want to get some influencers there to talk about Detroit and what the company is doing."

I hadn't lived in Detroit for years, but I needed the money, and it seemed doable. I started making calls to people I knew—or to anyone who knew someone who knew someone. Somehow, I pulled it off. I got people into that room, and for that effort, I made $3,000. That $3,000 felt like a lifeline; it meant I could pay my rent and bills for another month. The dinner was in November, on a cold and crisp night.

At that time, I was sober, but I was clinging to my sobriety by sheer willpower. I stepped outside for a cigarette—something I don't even do anymore—and ended up talking to a woman who had joined me. She might've been smoking too, or maybe she wasn't, but she was out there in the cold, just like me. We struck up a conversation, and at some point, she suggested we meet for breakfast the next morning. I said, "Sure, why not?"

I didn't think much of it at the time.

The next morning, we met at a small breakfast spot. As we talked, I learned that she was the head of marketing for the hotel where the dinner had been hosted. She also oversaw a group of hotels in cities like Omaha, Minneapolis and Indianapolis—smaller, less glamorous markets that still held their own charm.

Over breakfast, I kept the conversation light. I wasn't about to unload all my struggles onto her. She didn't need to know how much my life felt like it was crumbling beneath me.

Under the table, my knee was bouncing nervously as I tried to hold it together. All I could think was: *I've got to figure my life out.*

But somehow, in the midst of our conversation, a word slipped out of my mouth: "trudging." It wasn't a word I used often, but it holds deep meaning for me.

It's a term I'd learned from AA's Big Book, a sobriety bible for many people. The phrase "trudging the road of happy destiny" is all about the journey—about facing life's struggles head-on, one step at a time, even when the path ahead isn't clear.

At that point in my life, I felt like I was trapped in a forest, surrounded by falling trees. I couldn't see which way to go, and every direction felt like a dead end. I'd been having dreams about this forest, and when I woke up, I realized it was a metaphor for my life. I was losing so much—my stability, my sense of self—but somehow, deep down, I knew a path was being built for me. I just couldn't see it yet.

When I said "trudging," her face changed.

She looked at me and asked, "Are you sober?"

I hesitated for a moment but then said, "Yeah. I am."

She smiled knowingly and replied, "Me too."

Then she leaned in, her expression serious but kind, and asked me a question that changed my life forever: "How can I help you?"

That one word—"trudging"—opened a door I didn't even know was there. It was like the universe had been listening to my struggles and decided to give me a sign.

One word changed my life.

Her offer to help felt genuine, and it gave me a glimmer of hope that maybe, just maybe, I wasn't as lost as I thought.

That conversation marked a turning point. It didn't solve all my problems overnight, but it reminded me that even when life feels like it's falling apart, there are people willing to help. And sometimes, the smallest connection—a word, a moment of honesty—can change everything. That meeting wasn't just about breakfast or networking—it was a reminder that even in the darkest times, there's a path waiting to be discovered.

The Comeback Begins

The woman from the hotel group—I really and truly believe that there are angels in this world, and she was one of them—set me up hosting a series of trunk shows.

It tapped into my skills as a vintage and luxury expert, and it tapped into a growing market: I was selling to women who lived in cities like St. Louis and Omaha—Omaha was always really good to me—and Minneapolis, cities where there was real money but also a real dearth of luxury shopping opportunities. There was no Hermès store in Omaha, so the women who lived in Omaha turned to me. The concept was simple but genius—bringing luxury trunk shows to smaller cities where people didn't have access to these kinds of products.

That first show, which was held in Detroit, went well—I brought in stock, mainly Chanel and Hermès—and it was the start of something new. My friend even helped me name the brand: Covet by Christos.

At that first event, my Greek girlfriends and family showed up in full force, their support filling the room. That support got me through that month, both emotionally and financially. From there, I expanded to other cities, and suddenly, I was off to the races. I was so grateful—grateful for the second chance, for that spark that reignited my drive. I used the money to pay off some legal bills, cover my rent and even do a few fun things with Rolland.

Life wasn't easy, though. My days felt like a balancing act, just trying to keep my head above water. But I was determined. I told myself, *This is going to work. This will be the best business ever because it's mine.*

I traveled constantly, flying to Tennessee and Alabama and Missouri, finding ways to keep costs low, and selling whatever I could. My tenacity became my greatest strength. Slowly but surely, I started to rebuild—not just financially but spiritually, too. Work sometimes seemed like another addiction. It consumed me. Some days I felt like Walter Mitty, lost in a whirlwind of my own making. It was lonely—hotel rooms and long hours on the road—but I kept climbing.

By the end of 2018, I had built a business that grossed half a million dollars in its first year. The next year, I doubled that, grossing a million dollars. I wasn't personally making a million dollars on that, though—after expenses, I was left with just enough to pay rent, chip away at some debts and keep the lights on.

I met incredible people along the way, and they gave

me support that kept me going. The business continued to grow, and by February 2020, I hit a milestone: my best month ever, $200,000 in sales. At the same time, the stress, the constant travel and the endless cycle of selling and paying off debts were taking a toll. I was exhausted, and while I didn't want to admit it, the pace was killing me. Still, I pushed forward.

Then came March 2020.

I was on the road for another trunk show in Florida when I first heard whispers of something strange happening—a flu-like virus that hit hard, first in China and later, in Italy. At first, I didn't think much of it. I moved on to Chicago for a small show, staying at a hotel outside the city. That's when everything unraveled.

I got a message from the hotel: We're shutting down due to Covid. My mind raced. Panic set in as the reality of the situation began to sink in. My business depended on in-person events. If everything shut down, what would happen to me?

In that moment, I felt the weight of my world crashing down. February's $200,000 in sales suddenly didn't feel like an achievement—it felt like a liability. Consignment meant I owed $160,000 to other people, and the next month's bills were already looming. I stood there in that Chicago hotel room, trying to process it all, wondering how I was going to survive.

I remember the date, because how could I not: it was March 12, 2020, and the world as we knew it was about to change.

Rumors were swirling everywhere, and I was far from home, feeling increasingly anxious. Word had it that the

National Guard was going to close the borders around Chicago. My mind raced. I was stuck there in this hotel room—just me and a ton of Chanel. What was going to happen to me and my business?

Panic set in, but I knew I had to act fast. I had other friends in the resale business. We were all in the same boat, asking the same desperate question: "What are we going to do?" Out of options and short on cash, I applied for an immediate loan through Shopify. They approved me for $30,000 on the spot. *Great!* I thought. *I'll take it.*

The money hit my account, and I felt a brief moment of relief. But I knew survival required more than just funds.

I remember clutching onto a single glove I'd found, my pathetic attempt at staying safe from Covid. With that glove on, I hopped into a cab and made my way to Midway Airport. My plan was simple: get out of Chicago. But on the way, I got some devastating news—Midway Airport had shut down.

I sat there, stunned. Stranded in Chicago? Rolland was back in LA, my income had disappeared and I was completely out of ideas. But I wasn't ready to give up.

I redirected the cab to O'Hare and managed to book a first-class flight for just $110—no one was flying, after all. The airport was eerie, filled with people wearing masks. I remember thinking, *What the fuck is a mask even for?*

The flight itself felt surreal. It wasn't until I landed in LA that reality hit me full force. Rolland picked me up, decked out in a full HAZMAT suit. I couldn't believe my eyes. As I climbed into the car, it all sunk in: the world had completely changed.

At home, I stared at the wreckage of my once-thriving travel-based business. I had no website, no backup plan—nothing. It was just me, my dwindling resources and a rapidly changing world I didn't know how to navigate.

Looking back now, that moment marked another turning point. It was terrifying, surreal and chaotic. But it was also a testament to the sheer will to adapt, even when the odds seemed insurmountable.

I realized I had a choice: I could face everything with fear, or I could face it with faith. I knew deep down that fear wouldn't get me anywhere good. So, I made a decision. I had to let go of my anxieties and trust in something greater, something that would lead me toward a better outcome.

One of the most important things I've learned through my program is the value of staying focused on solutions, no matter what. It's not about having all the answers right away—it's about taking that first step, even when you're unsure of where it'll lead. It could be as simple as making a phone call or doing something small, but it's about moving forward, no matter how uncertain things seem.

That's where I started.

When I got home in March, I knew I needed to find a way to move forward. I wasn't sure what the answer was yet, but I knew I needed to take action. So, I went to a meeting. Honestly, I was afraid. But I also knew that speaking out loud, sharing my fears and being open to the unknown was the first step. I didn't have to have everything figured out, but I had to stay in motion and keep looking for solutions. In this moment, another angel came to me: I was doing a virtual event, and the subject of debt came up.

One of my clients reached out and offered to wipe out an amount that came to five figures in one fell swoop. I insisted on paying her back, but that gesture was a huge weight off my shoulders, allowing me to focus a little less on the troubles of the past and a little more on the opportunities of the future.

And something happened. Even though I was uncertain and scared, I kept pushing forward. I stayed in that mindset of finding a path forward, of thinking outside the box, and that's when things started to shift.

That's when I launched what would become my network as it exists today.

Looking back, it's clear that the fear could have stopped me, but it didn't. Instead, I chose to walk through it with faith, knowing that the first step would lead to something else. That's the power of staying in solution. It doesn't matter if you know the end result right away; what matters is that you keep moving forward.

Keep coming back.

Live, From The Closet, It's...

Another call I made in March of 2020 was to a creative friend, SJ. I was hoping our conversation would spark some kind of idea I could use to push forward.

"Christos," she said. "You need to go live...from the closet!"

I needed to go what from the where?

She was talking about Instagram Live, and the idea is that I'd bring the feeling of digging through celebrity closets in search of designer treasures—and funny stories—to social media.

On March 23rd, 2020, I relaunched my business. It wasn't just a relaunch—it felt like a desperate attempt to survive. I owed people money, I didn't know what to do next, but I had no choice. Sometimes, when your back is against the wall, you've got to make it happen. Oddly enough, the chaos in the world around me seemed to calm me down. For me, everything had slowed down. There was a strange stillness in the air, and in that silence, I found clarity. I could take a breath and figure things out. I went to a meeting online, and there, I prayed. I prayed for guidance, for the courage to do what I had set out to do.

I was going to start a live sales show. I would call it *Live In the Closet with Christos* and sell bags—sell anything, really—to keep the lights on and to pay my rent. At the very least, it would give me something to do.

I picked 5 pm LA-time for my first show because, I figured, it would be 8 pm on the East Coast and people would be done with work and dinner, looking for something to entertain them.

My grand plan was that 100,000 people would tune in. I came to this number by watching D-Nice, a pioneer of rap music and a hugely popular DJ. His Instagram Live shows had really taken off during the height of the pandemic, and hundreds of thousands of people tuned in to watch him. I could do it, too.

It was a tetherball moment all over again: I had a grand total of eight people watching (four of whom I'm sure were Russian bots, lol) for two hours. I didn't sell a single thing, but I just kept talking. I was figuring it out as I went along, and over time, my audience began to grow.

I was using what I had learned—everything from keeping people entertained and making them laugh to trying to sell things creatively. I didn't even know what I was doing half the time, but it didn't matter. I was determined. Years later, on the fourth anniversary of my business, I actually reached out to DJ D-Nice via social media, and, to my happy surprise, he responded. He joined me for an Instagram Live, and it felt like an amazing full-circle moment.

My follower count began to rise, and by the time I reached 25 viewers, I was thrilled. Twenty-five people watching my show felt like a huge win. I wasn't making a profit—actually, I was barely scraping by.

But every show was a small step forward.

I was figuring out how to sell and ship items from my tiny one-bedroom apartment. Every night, I hosted a show at 5 pm. Sometimes I did two shows a day. I even brought in friends whose stores had closed, helping them sell their items, but I wasn't financially benefiting from it.

It was all about building momentum. As the months went on, I grew more involved with Instagram. It became clear that it was the one social platform that *worked*, the one where I could begin to build a community.

I was still being shipped products from people I'd met, and one day, I misplaced a Chanel garment bag—a small thing, but it cost a lot of money. I posted a Story asking if anyone had an extra one.

Out of nowhere, a guy from Amsterdam replied. He told me he was a big vintage dealer and that he might have a garment bag I could use. He'd also been watching my live shows.

He asked me, "What do you charge for people to come on your show?"

I didn't even understand the question. Charge? Charge for what?

And then it hit me—a *Eureka* moment: I wasn't just selling things anymore. I was building a network.

I didn't need to sell products directly. I could bring people on the show, charge a fee for the appearance and just provide the entertainment, the platform and the authority. I set a price and we went live. It was just the two of us, no team helping me, no marketing in place. I had to do everything myself. But somehow, I made it happen.

That weekend, in just two hours, we did $100,000 in sales. And all I had to do was understand the market, bring people on the show and handle the invoicing. I earned 25 percent of the total. I sat there, stunned, thinking, *You just made $25,000 sitting on your couch talking about something you love.*

That was the moment I realized I had cracked the code. I was on fire. By the end of that year, I went from just me, hosting one show a day, to hosting five or six shows a day. The business was booming, and people were starting to take notice. It was a surreal feeling, watching everything grow, knowing that I had created something out of nothing.

In 2021, my business grew $15 million in sales in a single year—and it was just me. I hosted every single show, poured every ounce of myself into it and kept learning as I went along.

It was exhausting, it was thrilling and it was the most rewarding thing I'd ever done. I started moving and expanding, becoming more international. I picked up partners in London and Dubai, and I connected with sellers in Paris.

My vision wasn't just about resale and vintage items. It was about creating community. It was about understanding what people needed and delivering the products I loved to them. It could be vintage bags, beauty products or home decor—I'd post it all on my social media, and it was crazy. People just loved it, and I had no idea how big it was about to get.

At that point, I found out that live selling was already 30 percent of total retail sales in China, and here I was, surpassing Amazon in live selling. It was surreal. My life changed dramatically. I was live all the time, running the business non-stop. Rolland was the only person I talked to IRL most days, and even he barely saw me! But the upside? I was finally able to pay off my debts and start getting financially stable.

But even in the midst of success, a part of me felt like it could all be taken away at any moment. I thought about my dad, who had passed away at 59 with nothing to his name. That fear of losing it all—of losing everything I had worked for—drove me every day.

It was strange, though. In all the uncertainty, I felt like I had finally found my purpose. I was living my dream, building a business and making meaningful connections with people around the world. The community that had formed around my shows was incredible, and every day felt like a new opportunity.

In those quiet moments, when I would go for a walk and reflect, I'd wonder if this was real. *Was this really happening? Could this last?*

It was hard to comprehend, but deep down, I knew everything I had learned in my life—from my experience at HSN to my time at Clorox—was now coming together in this strange, unexpected way. I had become the showman I'd always wanted to be, weaving stories, entertaining and connecting with people in ways I had never imagined.

And in that moment, I knew that no matter what happened next, I had created something special.

The Comeback King Meets the Comeback Queen

If anyone has taught me—and the rest of the world—how to covet a comeback, it's Madonna. She's the comeback queen! Every time people have counted her out, she's come back with a new song, a new album, a new persona that makes people want more.

Since she first appeared on the scene, singing and

dancing and making it look effortless, I was completely obsessed with her. We were both from Michigan, and I think both of us had a similar sense of ambition and drive.

My first Detroit gay bar, Menjos, was hers, and we both went to University of Michigan. I would dream about her—like, literally dream. Back then, there was no internet, so my obsession was primarily fueled by whatever limited content I could find—anything Madonna-related, I was all over it.

I always had this deep-rooted belief that I would somehow meet Madonna someday. I even had these random premonitions from time to time. Once, I was in Chicago for work, and Madonna was filming *A League of Their Own* nearby. Naturally, in my mind, I was convinced that this would be the moment.

I turned to my partner at the time, James, and told him, “Madonna’s in town, and I’m going to meet her.” He just brushed it off, giving me a half-laugh of disbelief. Fine, whatever. But I just knew.

Fast forward to a casual dinner at this incredibly small Italian restaurant in Chicago. I was there with an old friend from college and his partner at the time—ironic considering we’d both dated the same girl back in the day, when we were both still “straight.”

We were sitting with our backs to the restaurant, and I was going on and on about Madonna throughout dinner, like a true fanatic. My friend’s new boyfriend—who by the way, I didn’t really like—decided to drop this absolute bomb on me: “You do realize she’s sitting two tables behind you, right?”

I'll never forget the moment I turned around.

There was Madonna, sitting just a couple of tables away. I felt my heart leap out of my throat. It was surreal. We left the restaurant for a moment to regroup, and I was literally jumping up and down outside, overwhelmed with excitement. I had to meet her, but what was I going to say? Should I just walk up and introduce myself? I needed a plan.

So, naturally, I came up with the idea to give her flowers. It made sense, right? A nice gesture to cushion the inevitable awkwardness. I dragged my friend to a nearby 7-Eleven, the only place open late, and bought a bunch of flowers that, admittedly, smelled like avocados. Not the greatest choice, but desperate times call for desperate measures.

Back we went to the restaurant, armed with these sad, avocado-scented flowers. Feeling nervous, I handed the flowers to my friend because—let's face it—if Madonna rejected me, I wouldn't be able to handle it. I was already on edge as it was. But, just like how he didn't follow through with his wedding to the boyfriend I knew he should break up with, my friend didn't follow through with the flowers either. "I can't do it," he said, freezing just steps away from Madonna, the person we were there for.

Typical.

So, there I was, clutching these 7-Eleven flowers.

I had no choice anymore.

Madonna saw me; I saw her. I approached and handed her the flowers with a somewhat mumbled,

"Madonna, we love you. These flowers are from someone up front."

Yeah, I couldn't even take ownership of the flowers! I was both excited and absolutely mortified. My clumsy friend then bumped into me like a fool, causing me to fall into—no, *literally* fall into—Madonna's lap.

I couldn't believe it. I was in Madonna's lap!

She looked down, probably a bit baffled, and just said, "Thank you."

I stammered something else and smiled awkwardly, feeling like my brain completely short-circuited. We eventually made it outside, and I was on cloud nine. The whole experience felt magical, like meeting royalty. For the rest of the night, I was floating in disbelief. I was that close to her!

For years, my obsession continued. I went to countless Madonna concerts, met people in her orbit and occasionally found myself just a few feet away from her backstage. But for some reason, I never approached her again. Part of me felt like that initial encounter couldn't be topped; part of me was just too anxious.

Then, five years ago, the unthinkable happened. Kelly —my best friend who I had first seen Madonna with back in the '80s during the Blond Ambition tour—called me up.

"Guess who's going to the Vanity Fair Oscars after-party with me?" she said. I almost dropped the phone. Kelly was now running Madonna's publicity team, and she told me, without a shadow of a doubt, "Christos, you're going to meet Madonna again tonight."

By this point, I had seen her live 33 times. You'd think I'd have my act together, but I was as much of a nervous wreck as ever. We got to the party, and I spotted Madonna walking down the hallway toward me. Kelly was escorting her, and I was just standing there, completely frozen.

Then it happened.

Kelly stopped, introduced me, and the Queen of Pop herself said, "Hi Christos, nice to meet you."

I was speechless. I had all these things I wanted to say, and instead, after all the years of idolizing her, all I could say was: "Gosh, you're pretty."

Madonna just smiled politely while inside I was dying of embarrassment. Kelly shot me a look that screamed, *Seriously? That's the best you could do?* But hey, what came out, came out. Sometimes you're just too starstruck to function like a normal human being.

We later ended up on the dance floor, swaying awkwardly alongside one another. But you know what? As nerve-wracking as it was, I had finally met the woman I had idolized my entire life again. And despite my bumbling awkwardness, it was everything I had ever wanted.

I may just be that geeky kid from Michigan who couldn't hold it together, but for me, Madonna has always been larger than life, something untouchable, and at the same time, deeply a part of my story. She still holds a special place in my heart, and she always will.

Maybe the third time will be the charm?

Chapter 10

For years after I first jumped headfirst into live selling, Covet by Christos began and ended with me. I was the star, the cameraman, tech support, the shipping coordinator (with the apartment Rolland and I live in doubling as the business warehouse). During each show, I'd keep track of who wanted to buy what so I could send invoices once we'd finished.

This obviously wasn't sustainable, and as the business grew, so did the team: I hired someone to help me take notes during shows, and then, slowly, I hired more trusted employees and show hosts, many of whom came to Covet by Christos as fans.

Today, I employ a team of almost 50, and I don't take that lightly: what was once an idea meant to help me make rent has grown into something that has allowed a *lot* of people to support their families, travel and grow their skillsets.

In 2022, we hit what seemed like an insane number at the time: $35,000,000 in sales. In 2024, we hit

$50,000,000, and by the time you're holding this book in your hands, Covet by Christos will have hit over $100,000,000 in lifetime sales. I still spend a lot of time working—like, all the time, actually.

Every day for me starts with a schedule, laying out anywhere from two to eight hours where I'm hosting different people on Instagram Live. I start by reviewing the list, making sure every guest meets their goals for the day.

While I'm live, I'm multitasking like you wouldn't believe—texts and emails flood in from my team with questions, updates and issues that need solving. And through it all, I've got to stay focused, energized and present for the audience. Lucky for me—or maybe not so lucky—I live in the same building where I work.

My home is just upstairs from the studio. The downside? I sometimes don't step outside for six days straight. There are times when I'm on a live session for six hours without a single bathroom break.

Imagine that—six hours of keeping up the energy, staying excited and giving 100 percent of myself. Between all that, there's planning: upcoming shows, new products, trips and live events. Then there's the big New York Fashion Week event I'm sponsoring, meetings with vendors, sorting through lists of people and products.

It's constant. And through it all, I'm making sure everyone's happy. That's a big deal for me—keeping people satisfied. I've built this brand on customer service, and I'm proud of it. My obsession with customer satisfaction comes from my background. I was trained by Disney, which taught me how to deliver exceptional experiences. Nobody does it like we do because, well, nobody can do it like we can. Seriously, I'm ruthless when it comes to customer care.

Amid all this chaos, I make sure to carve out time to work out every day. It's non-negotiable for me. But this pace takes a toll. I'm glued to my phone for at least 10 hours daily, typing constantly. And let me tell you, it's not without consequences. I've had a frozen shoulder from over-typing—trust me, it's the worst. And during the pandemic, I gained 40 pounds from being sedentary. I've since lost it, but it's a reminder of how this lifestyle can catch up with you.

I work alone most of the time, with a remote team scattered across the globe. Some of them, I've never even met in person. It's funny—I spend most of my day in meetings with myself, strategizing, brainstorming and yes, talking out loud like a madman. It's part of being an entrepreneur. You live and breathe your work. I wake up at five in the morning, and my mind is already racing with ideas. Gratitude is something I try to practice more, but it's hard when you're always in the thick of it.

I left the corporate world 25 years ago, but lately, I've found myself edging back into it. Corporate jargon—"alignment," "pain points"—makes me feel like I'm in a car dealership. It's ironic because all I wanted back then was to escape that world, and now here I am again, navigating it on my terms.

My pre-show routine is sacred. If I have a live show at 5 pm, I've got everything timed to the minute. At 4:51 pm, I jump into the shower while blasting "I'm Not in

Love" by 10cc. It's my thing. By 5 pm, I'm live and ready to go. It's a rush, really—always has been.

I've always felt like I was meant for something special. Even as a kid growing up in Detroit, in a chaotic household, I knew there was more out there for me. I wasn't the popular kid. I didn't fit in. But I had this drive to prove myself—to show the world I was capable of something bigger. When bullies would make fun of me, I'd somehow know, deep down, that they were wrong. That I was meant to be somewhere else, doing something important. That ambition fueled me through corporate life and beyond.

Listening to your inner voice is critical. It's guided me through the big decisions in my career. Acting on a gut feeling has led to some of the most transformative moments in my life. Like the time I was on a blind date in London and saw the Billboard magazine advertisement for my dream job. It felt like a sign, and I didn't hesitate—I went for it.

That's what I want people to understand: when opportunities present themselves, just jump. It might not be perfect, but perfection is overrated. Take the leap.

Of course, not everything works out. And when it doesn't, you have to look forward. Reinvention is key. When one door closes, another one opens, but only if you're willing to embrace what's next. Gratitude helps too. When life starts falling into place, it's easy to take it for granted. I've learned the hard way that staying grateful keeps everything from unraveling. Mental health is another cornerstone. Physical health is crucial, but your mental well-being is just as important.

Asking for help is something I've had to learn. It wasn't easy at first—I'm a proud person. But in sobriety, I realized it's okay to admit you're struggling. Whether it's asking for clarity in a meeting or reaching out during tough times, vulnerability is strength. Through it all, I've come to terms with something: not everyone is going to like you.

As someone who was Mr. Nice Guy growing up, always thoughtful, always putting others first, this was tough to accept. But it's liberating too. You can't please everyone, so you might as well focus on treating people right and staying true to yourself. Life's a balancing act—a constant dance between self-doubt and self-belief. Some days, that inner voice tells me I can conquer the world. Other days, it whispers that I can't. But I've learned to keep going, to push past the fear and to trust in the process.

The Stos Squad

I've sold a lot of valuable—and even priceless—treasures, but no *thing* could compare to the power of the Stos Squad.

I think this community formed because it wasn't just about selling and buying products—though that was certainly part of it. I'm a storyteller at heart, an entertainer who loves making people laugh. I can be a little sassy, and yes, I'm a good salesman too. This unique combination allowed me to envision something different: making shopping fun again, even in the midst of global uncertainty. I had this vision in my head about making it entertaining while showcasing products, trying to hold everything together when it felt like the world was falling apart.

When people look at the business valuation now and want to get involved, I always emphasize that it's the people first, the products second. Covet By Christos was conceived as an online network showcasing things I coveted—from resale items to everything else that makes life more exciting and fun. I wanted to bring content that entertained, host conversations with both famous and not-so-famous people, and make people laugh without the typical sales pitch. It wasn't just about the latest bag or beauty product—it was about creating an experience that made life a little more exciting and fun.

They're a loyal and committed group of people who prioritize togetherness above all else. The products? Those come second. We know each other's lives deeply—what's going on, who's new, who might need support. It's easy to spot someone new, and I'll ask, "Where are you from? Nice to meet you," and so it goes.

I have my own personal language: when a product comes up at a price I think is a great deal, I yell out, "Sit down, Bessie," as a nod to the days when my mom Aspasia (aka Bessie) was being cheered on by fellow Greeks at the bowling alley—because it was an automatic strike, like a "sold" on the network. It makes people laugh, and it's a fun way to bring a little bit of my mom's irrepressible spirit into each show.

The group is largely made up of women around my age, 30 to 65. Making new friends at this stage of life isn't easy. But somehow, we've built this community where real friendships thrive. We've traveled the world together, celebrated birthdays and rallied when someone gets sick. For someone like me, who's intrinsically a loner, it's nothing short of miraculous.

Loneliness is often a hallmark of people who've struggled with addiction like I have—alcoholism and drug addiction tend to push you toward isolation. Being part of this community feels like an act of contrary action, a complete departure from my natural inclination.

I've never been a "joiner." Even when I'm surrounded by people, I'm more of an observer, someone who prefers to be in the background. Yet here I am, engaging daily with this extraordinary group and stepping up in ways I never thought possible.

It's not always easy. Sometimes, I'm in a bad mood or overwhelmed by the demands of managing everything, and I carry that onto the show. But my community is there for me, just as I am for them. During the pandemic, we connected when isolation was at its peak. We've supported each other through illnesses like cancer, and simply shown up for one another. I became a steady presence, like a Johnny Carson type—a daily connection point, bringing some unpredictability and joy to our days.

The remarkable thing about this community was that it formed entirely virtually at first. Members knew each other only by their online monikers—"I Shop Forever 444" or "Shopping Piggy" or their children's names. Apart from a few people I knew from trunk shows in

Omaha, I hadn't met any of the thousands tuning in each week until July 2021.

Imagine building a community of thousands without ever meeting them face-to-face. It was unprecedented, yet somehow it worked.

Off Screen, In Real Life

The pandemic created this strange rhythm of lockdowns and brief openings, periods of isolation punctuated by possibilities for connection. When a brief window opened up during the summer of 2021, we seized the opportunity to meet in person. Someone suggested calling it "ChristosCon"—a name that made me laugh in disbelief.

Oh my God, are you kidding me? I'm going to name it after myself? I thought. But the name stuck, becoming a symbol of our growing community.

Our first gathering in Las Vegas brought together about 35 people, all carefully tested per COVID protocols. The moment these women who had never met in person walked into that room, it was electric.

"Are you Suzie 444? I'm Jenna 9999!"

These were well-heeled women letting loose with pure joy, creating pandemonium in the best possible way. I stood there, a bit awkward, watching these virtual connections transform into real-world friendships before my eyes.

Before leaving Vegas, I made an offhand comment about meeting next in Paris.

What are you saying, Christos? I thought to myself.

But sometimes the most audacious dreams have a way of manifesting themselves.

The following year, there we were—nearly 100 people cruising down the Seine, shopping in charming boutiques, sharing meals in beautiful locations. The movement was growing, taking on a life of its own. Each gathering seemed to build on the energy of the last, creating memories that would bind our community even tighter.

London followed, bringing even more incredible moments. During the planning stages, I casually asked, "I know this will never happen, but could we rent out Kensington Palace?"

It turned out we could. Then came another wild idea: "Is there any way I can get my logo on the building?" For $35 and a logo file, my company logo was projected onto Kensington Palace.

It was all surreal. This moment reminded me of one of life's most important lessons: if you don't ask for something, you already know the answer will be no.

Standing there that evening, watching my community members in black tie attire and evening gowns walking through the palace for a candlelit dinner, I couldn't help but marvel at how far we'd come from those solitary livestreams in my apartment. We had multiple events planned throughout London—the Prada Café, Kensington Palace and other extraordinary experiences that would have seemed impossible just a few years earlier.

Homecoming

This year, as I turned 60—a milestone I wasn't sure I'd reach, given my family history—I decided to take the community to Greece. This trip held special significance for several reasons. My father, uncle and grandfather on my dad's side had all died at 59, creating a shadow over my own mortality. Reaching 60 felt like breaking through a barrier, and I wanted to celebrate in a meaningful way.

The choice of Greece wasn't random. Eighty years ago, my parents had emigrated from there on a month-long boat journey, sick and uncertain about their future in America. Now here I was, leading a group of 100 people through Athens, sharing my heritage and connection to this land I'd visited almost yearly since age 15. It was a full-circle moment that would have seemed impossible to my parents when they first arrived in America.

Everything about the Athens trip exceeded expectations. We enjoyed a private fashion show by one of Greece's top haute couture designers, who spontaneously invited all 100 of us to her $48 million home afterward. Standing on her 5,000-square-foot balcony, we could almost touch the Acropolis. The impromptu nature of the invitation—with the designer casually suggesting we bring our food truck and DJ to her house—exemplified the magic that seems to follow our community wherever we go.

To make the moment even more special, I had spent months taking Greek lessons to deliver my opening speech in Greek. While most guests couldn't understand what I was saying, the meaning transcended language. Having my sister there to experience all the best parts of Athens, places I'd always wanted to see, made it even more meaningful. We had made my parents' homeland the backdrop for our latest adventure, and somehow it felt like they were there with us.

The End of the Beginning

This network has grown into something extraordinary. Together, we've raised half a million dollars for charity and created incredible memories and disrupted retail models. The connections I've made have even led to writing a book, which still feels surreal. It's an oh-my-God moment every time I think about it.

I've come so far from the darkest times in my life. I vividly remember sitting in my car in Hollywood, feeling a deep sense of doom. I was utterly defeated, questioning my worth and the choices I'd made. I felt I didn't deserve anything good. Back then, I even sabotaged opportunities because of that belief. Gratitude became my lifeline, and it's something I focus on every day now. Staying present, appreciating the journey—the good, the bad—it's what keeps me grounded.

My friend Kelly once told me something I'll never forget—that I always lead from my heart. Being Greek, it's in my nature. Sometimes it gets me in trouble, sometimes beautiful things happen, but it's who I am.

Four years ago, I was literally sitting in a closet, talking to my iPhone 12—the same phone I'm still using today because I consider it lucky. I showed up every single day, no matter what, and slowly built something meaningful. That experience taught me five critical lessons:

1. Show up. Consistency is everything.
2. Stay in the solution. When things go wrong, just take one step forward, and the universe will often handle the rest.
3. Practice gratitude. It's the key to staying present and appreciating the journey.
4. Trust your gut. While I have a strong left brain for numbers and strategy, I've learned to listen to my instincts.
5. Step back and reflect. Sometimes, I just need to pause and marvel at what we've built.

Of course, it hasn't all been smooth sailing. As someone who was severely bullied growing up, I'm naturally a people pleaser. Not everyone will like you, and I've had to accept that. But one of the biggest lessons I've taken from sobriety is the idea of keeping your own side of the street clean. At the end of the day, I can't control anyone or anything—a hard realization for someone who can probably be described as a control freak.

But through it all, I've come to understand the weight of my actions. The ripple effects of what I do touch so many lives, whether it's through the community I've built, the causes we've supported or the women I've mentored. Seeing their growth and success fills me with pride. I've become the rock they throw into the pond, creating ripples of change.

Financial security has played a role too, giving me the freedom to focus on what matters most—my loved ones, my community and my future. I've taken steps to ensure that my family won't ever have to worry about money, even if something were to happen to me. That peace of mind is invaluable.

My husband Rolland has been a rock for me through it all. We got married last February. On the surface, we seem like an unlikely match—I'm 60, he's 35. But none of that mattered when we met on Match.com in 2017.

At the time, I was at my lowest, both financially and emotionally. Rolland said he didn't know what the future held for me, but he's stood by me through everything. He's a fashionista, a churchgoer and someone who's sacrificed so much to support my work, even when it meant I couldn't always be as present as I wanted to be. I owe him so much, and I'm so grateful we found each other.

My sister René has also been a cornerstone of my life. We come from a small family, neither of us has kids, but we've always had each other's backs. René has supported me unconditionally, even when I was at my most vulnerable. In many ways, my journey has been a family effort, honoring the dreams of my parents, who saw potential in me and nurtured it. They worked hard and made sacrifices, and I feel like I'm making them proud.

At 60, I'm entering a new chapter, full of possibilities. I know there will be challenges, but I also know I'm ready for them. And as I reflect on where I've been and where I'm going, I'm filled with gratitude—for the struggles that shaped me, the people who supported me and the community that's become my family.

It's been a wild ride, and I can't wait to see what the future holds, because I know deep down it's going to be good. That's the power of the comeback: it is what you want it to be.

So covet it. Covet the comeback.

You have nothing to lose.

Epilogue

As a proud Greek, I couldn't write this book without an epilogue. It's technically our word for "conclusion," but I don't think it's entirely fair to call this a conclusion. In telling my story, I'm kicking off a new chapter: one where my goal is to help others see that a comeback is always possible, and that the struggles you face today don't have to define what tomorrow looks like.

I wrote this book sitting in my home in LA, looking out at the Hollywood Hills and thinking about everything they—and I—have seen. Rolland was often in the next room, popping in and out to say hello, his love and our life together serving as something happy to come back to when writing took me deep in the weeds of my darkest days.

Looking back on my journey, I realized that life is a series of highs and lows, victories and setbacks, each one leading to the next. They were simply moments along the path, seasons that came and went, each with its own lessons. There were times when I felt invincible, riding the wave of fame, but just as quickly, those waves would crash, humbling me and bringing me back to earth. Navigating these cycles taught me resilience—not in clinging to success or fearing failure, but in accepting that both were part of the story and both made me who I am today. I'm grateful to the tetherball, even though those whacks to the face were pretty painful.

It wasn't all bad, though: I've learned so much from people like my parents, Richard Branson, Mickey and Minnie Mouse and—of course—Madonna. I've made friends who I know will be by my side for the rest of my days, as I will be there for them. I've also learned that I have the capacity to make new friends and to feel comfortable really showing my full self to other people, even though I'll always be a Gemini at heart.

I've also accumulated a *lot* of good material, and believe me: what isn't in this book could easily fill a sequel. And maybe it will.

After all, aren't Greeks the expert when it comes to epic sagas?

Acknowledgments

To my husband Rolland, who has been my rock and divine presence since day one.

To my sister René, who keeps me on the straight and narrow and doesn't let me forget about it.

Thank you to God and those with me on my sobriety journey.

To my best friends Kelly, Linda, Katie, Garcelle, Nikki, Harlan, Brett and Michael—thank you for being there for thick and thin and back again.

To my team at Legacy Launch Pad, especially Anna David who took a chance on me in an instant and my writing partner Angela Serratore, who got me and my voice.

To Amber, who changed my world with one word.

To #stossquad, thank you to each and every one of you for coming along on this crazy magical journey with Covet by Christos.

Nick and Aspasia: this Greek boy thanks you for everything.

About the Author

Christos Garkinos is a fashion entrepreneur, social commerce innovator, television personality and author. Born to Greek immigrant parents in Detroit, he worked with industry giants including Disney and Virgin Megastores before launching his own successful fashion line on HSN. Garkinos was a pioneer in the luxury resale business and the star of a Bravo TV show. He has been featured in *Vogue*, *Harper's Bazaar* and *The New York Times* and founded Covet by Christos, a $100 million dollar luxury live-streaming network and community platform. Garkinos lives in Los Angeles with his husband, Rolland. *Covet the Comeback* is his first book.

Legacy Launch Pad is a boutique publishing company that works with entrepreneurs from all over the world.

For more information about Legacy Launch Pad Publishing, go to: www.legacylaunchpadpub.com.

www.ingramcontent.com/pod-product-compliance
Lightning Source LLC
Chambersburg PA
CBHW051139250325
24043CB00036B/524
* 9 7 8 1 9 6 4 3 7 7 3 4 6 *